Published in January 2007

British Library Cataloguing in Publication Data:
A catalogue record for this book is available from the British Library

ISBN 978-1-84425-319-7

Published by Haynes Publishing, Sparkford, Yeovil, Somerset BA22 7JJ, UK
Tel: 01963 442030  Fax: 01963 440001
Int. tel: +44 1963 442030
Int. fax: +44 1963 440001
E-mail: sales@haynes.co.uk
Website: www.haynes.co.uk

Haynes North America Inc.
861 Lawrence Drive, Newbury Park,
California 91320, USA

Printed and bound in Great Britain by
J. H. Haynes & Co. Ltd, Sparkford

# The Camping Manual

Peter Frost

## The step-by-step guide to camping for all the family

# Contents

## Introduction

## 1 The tents

## 2 Trailer tents and folding campers

## 3 Other equipment

# 4 Going camping

# 5 Some other ways to go camping

# 6 Where can you do it?

# 7 More information

# Why go camping?

If you want the freedom to go where you like when you like with no need to book…

*…then go camping.*

If you want to take your family on holiday, buy all the equipment you need and pay what you would for a fortnight in a hotel in Spain, but have your tent and other camping equipment for breaks and holidays for the next five years at least…

*…then go camping.*

If you want to wake up to a dawn chorus rather than an alarm clock and smell the dew on the grass through your tent door as you look out on the best view you've seen this month…

*…then go camping.*

If you don't want all the petty rules and regulations of a hotel or guesthouse, but want to get up when you want, go to bed when you want, eat when you want, and wear what you want…

*…then go camping.*

If you want to fly off on a cut-price airline with all your accommodation on your back for a cheap stay in places as exotic as Iceland or Croatia, or as popular as the French Riviera or the Costa del Sol…

*…then go camping.*

Remember those great times? Your first camping trip with the Scouts or the Girl Guides? If you want to relive them and recreate those innocent times…

*…then go camping.*

If you want the best seats near the best stages at the best festivals, and want to stroll back to bed when the evening's excitement is over…

*…then go camping.*

# Why do so many people go camping?

If you ask keen campers why they love it, you'll get a dozen different answers. But one word will crop up over and over again: freedom. The freedom to go where you like, usually without having to book. To chase the good weather. If it's raining in Wales, head for East Anglia. If the TV weather forecast says that it's better in the north than the south, then you can head north.

Freedom is important when you're actually on site. Get up early, if that's what you want to do, or lie in till lunchtime – you certainly won't be the only one doing so on most campsites.

You can eat when you like too – an early breakfast or a mid-morning brunch that turns into a long and well lubricated lunch. When you're on a campsite, mealtimes are entirely up to you.

And you can do what you like. You can relax outside your tent with a cup of coffee, a small beer or a glass of wine, you can read, or you can just enjoy the view – on a campsite it's entirely up to you.

When all that relaxing has exhausted you, you might want to try something a bit more active. Camping and walking

always go together and whether it's a slow meander to the local pub or a vigorous hike to the summit of those distant hills, you'll find that your own tent on a comfortable campsite makes the perfect base for any kind of outing.

If you want to roam further you'll find many campers are keen cyclists. Again, your campsite will be the gateway to some healthy and fascinating cycle routes.

Another reason why people camp is the cost. Camping can provide some of the least expensive holidays you'll ever experience. That means you can go

further and stay longer than you could using more expensive kinds of accommodation. Book a hotel holiday in Spain, for instance, and you get to use the hotel room for just the week or two you've booked it. Buy a tent and it's not yours for just two weeks, but for countless holidays and short breaks for years to come.

Once you've bought your camping equipment, then assuming you look after it following some of the maintenance tips given in this book you'll be amazed just how long it will last and how many holidays and short breaks that will represent. Your tent will take you for a fortnight's holiday somewhere in sunny Europe, to the Lake District for an early Spring walking holiday, and to that music festival you've always promised yourself.

Tents come in handy for dozens of things. For fishing expeditions, for visiting friends and family, and for all the other times you just want to get away for a few days.

The purpose of this book is to tell you everything you need to know to start family camping: what to buy and what not to buy, how to make sure you get the right tent, how to get together all the accessories you need to be really comfortable on your holiday, and how to look after your kit.

What you won't find in this book is a lot of stuff about expeditions to the ends of the earth or the summits of mountains. We won't be taking you to the North Pole or to the fiery deserts of Africa. But here's a comforting thought – whenever brave explorers set off to such terrifying destinations they usually take a tent, and if it's good enough for them then it's certainly going to be safe enough and comfortable enough for you and your family.

**Opposite:** With a good tent and the right kit the world is your oyster.

**Right:** A real campfire – the perfect end to a day on the open air.

# Camping – the green holiday option

There's no doubt at all that camping is the most environmentally friendly holiday you can have. David Bellamy, perhaps Britain's best-known environmentalist, has declared campsites to be 'oases of bio-diversity'.

Campsites leave the smallest environmental footprint on the land they use. If you build a hotel you cover up the grass and the trees with concrete. If you build a campsite you leave the ground pretty much as it is. This means that campsites remain friendly environments for birds, animals, and plants, and campers get the chance to share their holiday locations with some interesting flora and fauna.

When you're camping you really communicate with nature. You'll be woken by the dawn chorus. Town dwellers won't believe just how many birds sing out in the morning, and you'll soon learn who the early risers are and who joins the chorus at a more civilised hour.

Campsite owners plant thousands of

just how environmentally friendly it can be.

The *Guardian* newspaper asked of the Camping and Caravanning Club site at Windermere, 'is this the greenest campsite in Britain?' The club, with help from its President David Bellamy, has tried to redevelop the site with the minimum of impact on the beautiful countryside of the Lake District.

All the roads and buildings on site are built from local stone. Not only do they look at home in the local environment, but they also reduced the amount of carbon dioxide produced in transporting raw materials to the site.

Weather in the Lakes can be wet. At Windermere the club harvests all that rainwater. A huge underground tank – as big as a house – stores the rainwater, which is used throughout the season for flushing toilets.

The toilets are lit not by electric lights but by Suntubes – clever mirrored tubes in the roof that illuminate the shower and toilet blocks even on the

trees and shrubs on their sites every year. One site can have as many as 10,000 trees and shrubs planted to enhance its landscape.

Campers score well when it comes to other forms of environmental impact too. Although many arrive by car, once on site most will dig out their walking boots or take to bikes to get around. Another victory for the environment.

Let's visit a typical campsite and see

**Left:** Recycled plastic gratings are filled with soil, fertilizers and grass seed to create grass surfaced hard standings suitable for tents as well as other camping units.

**Above:** Share your holiday site with the butterflies.

**Right:** The Club plants literally thousands of trees and shrubs on its sites every year.

dullest day. Water for the showers is heated by efficient gas heaters that generate the minimum of emissions.

As well as utilising these high tech contributions to the environment the club has planted thousands of native trees and shrubs to ensure that, visually, the site makes a positive contribution to this corner of Lakeland.

Campers do their bit to preserve our fragile environment too. We've already talked about reducing the use of cars by walking and cycling. To that should be added the lower amount of energy that the average camper will use during a stay on site. Less water, less electricity, less pollution. Campers really do leave a small and insignificant environmental footprint.

And so they should, for much of the joy of camping comes from enjoying that natural environment. When you share your home with the deer, the squirrels, the woodpeckers and the dragonflies you'll really learn to appreciate them and soon learn to look after the campsite. Remember, it is your home for the weekend but their home for life.

David Bellamy was born in London and as a teenage boy he discovered what he calls his 'Swallows and Amazons Camping' in the Lake District, taking his drinking water from the Lakes and living beside the water in a small tent. Today, almost 60 years, on he still waxes eloquently about feeling the wet grass under his bare feet and smelling dew in the early morning. Of all types of holiday camping has changed the least.

In a countryside that is constantly changing, and not always for the better, camping has the least impact and offers the best chance of enjoying it without spoiling it.

**Right:** On some sites the Club has created wildlife ponds that make a great place to sit quietly to watch water birds and dragonflies.

# A little history

Today the vast majority of the world's tents are made in China – which is quite appropriate, for almost certainly it was the Chinese who invented tents, and they've been making them for at least 3,000 years.

Of course, early tents weren't holiday accommodation. People lived in them, and even today the planet's great nomadic tribes still make their homes in traditional tents. The yurts of Mongolia and the tipis of the Native Americans are just two famous examples.

Leisure camping, however, is considerably younger. It probably started in Britain, although some Americans would argue with that: and it happened in the latter half of the nineteenth century. Certainly the world's first camping club had been formed by 1901 – and it's still going strong today. Increasingly Edwardian gentlemen, and just a few ladies, were discovering the joys of camping as a way of experiencing open-air life. Its popularity grew.

There was no commercial camping equipment and early campers had to make their own. They often designed it themselves, and gradually some of their designs became available commercially.

In 1914 came the First World War. As is so often the case, the clouds of war had just a little silver in their lining: the conflict saw many men visiting distant places and living under canvas.

Many, sadly, didn't return, and a lot of those who did never wanted to see a tent again. A few, however, had discovered the excitement of travel and seeing foreign places, and realised that camping was a way to experience such

things for pleasure. A bonus was the mass of surplus army equipment that became available in the post-war period, so that those with a few bob found they could equip themselves economically and go out and enjoy the countryside, at home and abroad.

Commercial and club campsites were established – indeed, the Camping Club obtained its first campsite in 1914 at Walton on the banks of the River Mole in Surrey, and a group of members

**Above:** On honeymoon in the 1920s. Mr and Mrs Callander from Lancashire look comfortable.

**Left:** Cycle camping around 1910. H Winton Wood and J.H. Wood in a home made tent. J.H. would go on to design one of the most famous tents ever – the Itisa.

travelled to Holland on the Club's first overseas camping tour the same year. The holiday camping boom had started.

During the 1920s and 1930s camping and enjoying the outdoors became popular with the middle classes. Bikes, motorbikes, and cars were appearing on the roads of Britain in ever-increasing numbers, and the freedom they offered could be extended by taking your camping gear with you for a weekend away.

Then the lights went out all over Europe, and with the outbreak of the Second World War armies once again toured the globe living in tents. The situation at the end of the war was a repeat of that found after the First World War. Men – and some women – in the Armed Forces had learnt how to look after themselves in camps, and when hostilities ceased some of them found they could enjoy cheap holidays using camping equipment purchased from the many high street shops established to sell army surplus gear.

Out of the austerity of the 1950s came the boom of the 1960s. Colourful frame tents arrived from France, and camping kits were offered by firms like Headquarters & General. These kits included everything a family needed for a camping holiday.

Camping holidays grew in popularity, but on the horizon were cheap flights and the wall-to-wall hotels of the Spanish Costas. But enthusiasts remained faithful to camping, and there were lots of them. They began to discover the giant and sophisticated campsites of sunny Europe.

Today, tents and camping are booming again. Airport queues and substandard resort hotels have made package holidays less attractive, and more and more people are discovering what camping has always had to offer. You can sum it up in one word: freedom.

**Right:** The Itisa remained popular for many years.

## The man who started it all

Thomas Hiram Holding is generally reckoned to be the man who started leisure camping. This millionaire Edwardian Mayfair tailor designed the first lightweight tents. He made them in oiled silk and they used telescopic bamboo poles.

Holding lectured on camping at the turn of the twentieth century. For his lectures he would wear a Norfolk jacket and from its many pockets he would take out his lightweight and exquisite equipment to illustrate his camping tips.

He had led an interesting life. In his teens his parents took him to America and across the Prairies to Salt Lake City in Utah. They ate buffalo, fought off Indians, and his parents ran over him with their covered wagon! Their return journey was via the Rockies.

Back in England, Holding never got his love of the great outdoors out of his system. A keen cyclist, he founded the Cyclist Touring Club (CTC). which is still the premier organisation of its kind in Britain.

In 1901 Holding and five friends cycled to Wantage. They camped overnight, and while sitting round the campfire they resolved to form a club. It started as the Association of Cycle Campers, became the Camping Club, and is today known as the Camping and Caravanning Club. It has 400,000 members, about a hundred thousand of whom still camp in tents of various kinds.

# The tents

1

## What a choice

It's hard to believe that there are over a thousand
makes and models of tent on sale in Britain today. Go
along to an outdoor camping exhibition and the
choice will amaze you. There are ridge tents, dome
tents, tunnel tents, and frame tents. Different designs
and the same designs in different fabrics. New season
colours and the latest technical features.

In the next few pages we'll try and take you
through the various shapes, and their advantages and
disadvantages. We'll look at tents large and small, and
what you need to look for in order to get a tent that
suits you.

# Choosing your tent: the full story

Choosing your tent is the key decision for successful camping. Here we set out the basic questions you need to ask yourself when deciding on the perfect tent.

## Judge the quality

It's difficult to grade quality in tents. Certainly *The Camping Manual* isn't able to tell you which are the best tents to buy. This depends on many things – not least on price, of course, and personal preference plays an enormous part too.

The Consumers' Association tests tents and other camping equipment, and the results of their independent and rigorous tests are published in *Which?* magazine. In a recent round of tests Wild Country made the best tunnel tent on test. Sunncamp, Vango, Khyam, and Peakland were the best buys in other categories. Coleman made the best sleeping bag on test and Campingaz were the best buy among inflatable beds.

Full reports are available from the Consumer Association, and no doubt *Which?* will be looking at camping equipment again in future issues.

**Left:** This small and simple dome tent is ideal for backpackers.

**HOW BIG DOES IT NEED TO BE?**
The size of a tent is normally described in terms of the maximum number of people it will sleep. A two-berth or a ten-berth? Sounds simple doesn't it, but it needs more than a little thought.

Remember that you need space in your tent for more than just sleeping. Over the years we've found that four-berth tents work really well for two adults, and larger tents can work well for families. Two children will often be much happier if they've each got their own sleeping compartment.

But don't go mad. The bigger the tent is, the harder it generally is to put up, and the more space it will take in the car. You can buy huge and relatively inexpensive tents these days and beginners are often tempted by what seems like a great bargain, only to find out later how annoying it is to erect the huge palace in which they'll only use half the space.

The size of a tent will also affect its weight. Some large tents are really heavy, and whether you're backpacking or using a car or a trailer, make sure you're happy with lifting the tent that you intend to buy. Also consider its packed size. Those giant tents can be big to store and take up lots of space when they're in their one or more packing bags.

A most important aspect of size, however, is headroom. Smaller tents don't offer standing headroom, but it's great to be able to stand up straight in the morning, even just to pull your trousers on. Check that out when you see your intended purchase erected – as you certainly should. Never buy a tent from a picture in a catalogue.

**WHY DO TENTS HAVE TWO LAYERS OF FABRIC?**
Not all do. Very light weight small tents can be single layered, so can some larger tents. For the family camper all serious tents will have inner and outer layers. Check the gap between the two. Enough room to put your hand in as a fist is probably about right: don't buy a

tent where the inners and outers touch – that will certainly cause leaking on cotton tents.

Many smaller tents are pitched with the inner first and then a flysheet is added for weather protection. In larger tents you often put up the outside first and then fit a number of inner tents that define how you use the space inside.

Today, most tents will have a fitted (sewn-in) groundsheet. In smaller tents it will cover the whole of the inner tent floor, but in larger family tents each compartment will often have its own groundsheet.

Check the strength of the groundsheet material. In a good tent there will be an edge that stands up to make the whole bottom of the tent waterproof.

## WHAT SHAPE SHOULD MY TENT BE?

The shape will be important. Will it be a dome, a tunnel, a cabin, or a frame tent? Will it be a hybrid? We'll take you through all the shapes step-by-step later in this chapter.

## WHAT SHOULD MY TENT BE MADE OF?

Tents can be made of cotton canvas, nylon, or polyester. Poles can be of aluminium or composites. We look at tent fabrics in detail on page 48, and poles are dealt with on page 50; and while we're at it you'll find details of pegs, guy ropes, and groundsheets on pages 56 and 57.

One thing to watch is that some tent designs are made in more than one fabric. This will affect both price and performance.

## WHAT ABOUT DOORS AND WINDOWS?

Ventilation is very important in a tent so you'll need to have a good look at doors and windows. Some doors also act as a windbreak and some double as a canopy, to give you extra space under cover but still in the open air – ideal sometimes for cooking.

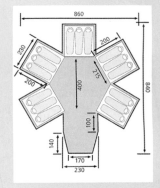

## Wot? No footprints?

Tent brochures, websites, and point-of-sale materials in camping shops are full of tent floor plans, or 'footprints' as the trade likes to call them. At their best they are pretty pictures giving a fair hint as to the size of a tent. At their worst they are fraudulent deceptions akin to the artist's impressions once so beloved by the disreputable end of the package holiday brochure business.

You will not find any footprints in this book.

The problem, of course, is that they take no account of real people and the various sizes in which they come. Nor do they consider how tents are used in the Real World.

In fact they're another good argument to see the tent you're thinking of buying actually erected. Climb inside, all of you who're going to use the tent. Lay down where you'll be sleeping. If it's big enough have a little walk about. Where will you cook? Will the children be under your feet?

If you all fit and reckon you could live in the space then add that model to your list of potential purchases.

---

Check door zips. Good tents will have double pulls so that you can open a door from the top or the bottom. And check that there is a way of rolling the door back and fixing it. Some tents will have porches, and again you need to make sure that it all works well and that the space is useful to you.

Now check the windows. They need to make the inside light and airy and should have mosquito nets so that even when the window is open you'll still get a midge-free night's sleep. On warm nights you'll certainly want to sleep with the door and windows open and the midge nets in position.

Finally, if you can, watch an expert putting your chosen tent up, and better still have a go at it yourself. It's a great way to see just how well a tent is designed and made. Although it's not always possible to see your chosen tent erected it's always worth asking the person selling the tent before you make your final decision.

**Below:** This tunnel tent offers good standing headroom and a great porch.

# The shape of tents

**Above left:** A simple timeless ridge tent. Doing its job today as well as ever.

**Above right:** This otherwise basic dome tent adds another flexible pole to make a useful porch.

**Below:** Tunnels work well in all sizes.

Once upon a time all tents were – well, not to put too fine a point on it – tent-shaped. They had a pole at each end and sometimes a cross pole called a ridge holding up a tent-shaped roof.

Ridge tents are remarkably stable and range from tiny one-person tents right up to large marquees. They are easy to pitch and still make excellent shelters today. However, disadvantages of their roof shape are the lack of headroom near the sides and the fact that the poles in the middle of the entrance always seem to be in the way. In order to get round this problem the single

pole can be replaced by an 'A' frame arrangement of two poles, but two poles are heavier than one.

Poles for ridge tents were first made of wood, or, for lightweight tents, bamboo. Then metal poles became the norm. These were made of steel or, later, aluminium – both heavy for the size of tent, although steel was much heavier than aluminium.

Finally there came the bendy pole, and dome tents became fashionable. Flexible poles still rule today. The basic principle involved bending a flexible pole into a half circle and fixing both ends to a strong tape or webbing strap that ran across the base of the tent, often as part of the groundsheet. Two flexible poles crossing in the middle gave a square dome, three poles a hexagon. The sides were more vertical, so overall headroom was better across a wider floor area. Stability was good in small tents, but unlike the ridge-tent design domes could become less stable as they got bigger.

The next step in tent-shape evolution sounds highly technical: the geodesic and the semi-geodesic style. Long and very impressive words, but all they actually mean is that, unlike dome tents, where the poles always cross in the middle at the top, the poles cross lower down and more often, thus making a better braced structure and a more stable tent. Geodesic and semi-geodesic designs are still popular, particularly for smaller tents and especially in those meant for more challenging camping environments.

Since domes don't necessarily provide the most usable space, another way of using flexible poles was to stand them up in a line to create a tunnel tent.

Once domes and tunnels started to grow in size, tent designers started to add extra rooms to the basic structure. The trend started in France, where a large central part of the tent offered standing headroom and a room off each side provided two sleeping compartments. These two compartments faced one another – in other words they were face to face, hence their French description of *vis-à-vis*. Interestingly vis-à-vis tents could be domes or tunnels, and indeed, some of the very first ones were in fact square frame tents.

The designers came up with ever more complex designs and scaled up their favourite small tent shapes into

bigger and bigger family tents. Different companies would take a close look at what their rivals were doing, and a new and popular shape one year would be in everybody's range the next, and generally sizes would grow.

But not all designs worked as well in different sizes, and scaling up was not always a good idea. Some very unstable giant domes were produced, while, generally speaking, tunnels worked better in bigger sizes. However, there are plenty of tents out there to disprove both of those generalisations.

Our American friends tended to stick with rigid poles, particularly for larger tents. They built square frames for their tunnels, and these have since crossed the Atlantic and are becoming popular in Europe. Over here we tend to call them cabins but this description is far from universal.

The flexible pole hasn't swept all before it. Frame tents still exist and remain popular. They use a rigid framework of straight poles (usually steel) with angled joints and can offer lots of space, including good headroom. They tend to be heavier and take somewhat longer to put up than other tents, but they're very stable when erected properly.

Finally, we mustn't forget trailer tents, the best of which constitute the luxury end of tented accommodation. Trailer tents and folding campers have their own section in *The Camping Manual*, beginning on page 58.

**Above:** This vis-à-vis tent has a dome at its centre and two tunnel extensions for sleeping.

**Left:** Frame tents have changed little in decades. That's because they still offer roomy comfortable camping. They come in a range of sizes from our small example here to some real giants.

**Below:** Trailer tents have their own section of *The Camping Manual*. It starts on page 58.

# Small is beautiful: more small tent tips

The choice of small tents is huge. It's possible to pop in to your local High Street catalogue store and buy what they'll describe as a small disposable tent and still get change from a £10 note! Such a tent will probably do you for a couple of nights at a summer festival or for the kids to try camping in the back garden on a summer's night.

Pay nearly 30 times as much and you can own what the *Guinness Book of Records* describes as the lightest small tent in the world, the Terra Nova Laserlite Competition. The Laserlite comes in an unbelievably small package and weighs, with poles, pegs, and inner tent, less than a bag of sugar. It will take you to a high mountain-top and bring you back safely, yet you'll hardly notice it in your rucksack.

In fact if you're prepared to settle for a single skin you can prove the *Guinness Book of Records* wrong and find an even lighter tent, such as this Raid from Coleman.

Unless every gram is that important to you, you'll probably settle on something a little less extreme. There are hundreds of small tents to choose from, like the simple dome tent on the page opposite.

As with all kinds of tents, you can find a variety of qualities and prices when shopping for a small tent. Virtually all of them are sewn in China but quality and design can vary enormously between different brands.

Another thing that seems to vary between brands is just how big manufacturers think their particular customers are. You'd think all two-berth tents would be the same size and actually have two berths. Wrong! Some two-berths would be hard pushed to take the average couple unless they were very friendly indeed. Others are just plain cosy.

If weight and packed size are not the most important factors in your choice we'd always recommend choosing a tent with one or two more berths than you think you need. Weight and size are less important if you're travelling by car, not least because you'll be able to store the kit you don't need overnight in your vehicle.

## Kit out with a kit

Many people will buy their first tent as part of a complete kit. Most outdoor and camping shops, particularly the big chains, will have beginners' camping kits for one or two people.

A one-person kit will include a small dome or simple tunnel tent, a sleeping bag, a basic sleeping mat, and a rucksack to carry it all in.

For two people the tent will probably be the same model, but there'll be two sleeping bags and mats and the rucksack will be replaced by a large holdall.

At the start of the season and during festival time price wars can develop between shops. Then £50 will buy a reasonable kit for two, and if you have a hundred to spend the world is your oyster.

Better, more expensive kits are available, but there's much to be said for starting out with a basic starter kit to discover if you're really going to enjoy camping.

Watch out too at some of the budget supermarket chains. Aldi, for instance, sometimes offer beginners' camping kits at unbelievable prices.

## A tent of a different colour

What appears to be the same small tent can often be found in different colours, made from different fabrics, or with poles of different materials. These differences can affect performance, weight, and, of course, the price you pay.

This is particularly important if you're choosing from a picture in a catalogue or on a website. Are you really comparing like with like?

You'll also find identical tents bearing different brand-names in different outlets. All of the large High Street camping shops with multiple branches have their own brands. Gear sold under these brand-names can either be of their own design and manufacture or else rebranded from another maker's range.

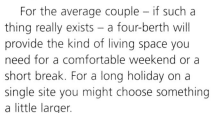

For the average couple – if such a thing really exists – a four-berth will provide the kind of living space you need for a comfortable weekend or a short break. For a long holiday on a single site you might choose something a little larger.

Other space issues with small tents involve finding the room for storage and cooking. The answer to both problems is often the porch. A good porch design is certainly just as important as the size and shape of the sleeping area.

It's never safe to cook in a small tent. Good advice, true, but you may be reluctant to take it when you're cold, hungry, and it's chucking it down outside. That's when a good porch like the one on this small Vango dome will prove its value.

An even larger porch, as in this tunnel, also from Vango, will give you somewhere to cook, and even provide the dog with somewhere to sleep.

Outwell have gone even further with the curvy and stylish awning pictured here.

## Following fashion?

Perhaps one of the most unexpected things to have happened to camping in the last year or so is that it has become involved with the world of high fashion. We know camping has always been cool, but when no less an authority than *Vogue* magazine tells you so – and takes a full-page fashion feature to do it – you'd better believe it.

Perhaps that's what inspired High Street camping chain Millets to get leading fashion designer Cath Kidston to design a range of colourful print tents and other camping kit.

Another well-known outdoor chain, Blacks, bought in Ted Baker, and he too has produced designs that will turn a few heads on the average campsite.

Some small-tent campers increase their available space with what is known as a tarp. Originally this would have been a small tarpaulin or industrial cover. Today it could be a purpose-made camping tarp, but is just as likely to be a lightweight groundsheet, or simply a sheet of waterproof plastic. Rigged with a couple of spare poles and a few guy lines and pegs, it provides shelter from the rain and shade from the sun. Coleman has moved the concept on by making the simple tarp an elegant extension to their tent range.

## Some other features to check out

The key feature in the design of any tent is ventilation. Has the tent you're looking at got plenty? This one from Outwell certainly has.

Windows too are important if you want light inside. They're even more important if your tent is made of a dark fabric. Again, a good example comes from Outwell.

Are the tiebacks for the doors simple ribbons? These elasticated toggle ties from Sunnflair are much better.

Windows, doors, and ventilators alike need to be screened against midges and mossies if you want to enjoy a good night's sleep. As someone once said in another context altogether: 'If you think you're too small to be effective you've never slept with a mosquito.'

One great bonus of really small tents can be found at some large and busy sites like the Camping and Caravanning Club site on the edge of Derwentwater, where a camping lawn that runs down to the beach is reserved for very small tents. This is the best part of the site and it's a great feeling to lie in you tent (particularly if it only cost a tenner) and watch night fall across the lake and over the fells beyond. Even better is knowing that the folk behind you in their motorhomes and caravans that cost thousands haven't got half as good a pitch or view as you.

## Now that's what I call a shopping trip

Here's a great tip for an exotic camping experience. Your author and his wife have had several camping holidays to various destinations in the USA. We buy a cheap flight and add a hire car package. We pack light, with lots of space left in our bags for the inevitable shopping you can't resist across the Atlantic. We take no camping equipment. When we arrive our first night is usually spent in a motel.

After a good night's sleep we're off to find the best camping store in town. We know we're sure to find one, because the Americans love their camping. The choice of kit is mind-boggling, the quality superb, and the prices cheap – roughly in dollars what we'd expect to pay in pounds in the UK. After a great holiday the choicest camping items go home in our luggage. Bulky items we drop off at a homeless centre or a charity store.

We bought our first complete camping kit at a store in Phoenix, Arizona, more than a decade ago. It cost under $50 and served us well pitched on the ridge of the Grand Canyon. Ten years on we're still using the enamel cowboy coffee pot that came as part of that kit. Holiday souvenirs just don't get any better.

# Putting up a lightweight champion

The Raid from Coleman is one of the lightest tents you'll find. It weighs less than a bag of sugar and makes a reasonable shelter for two friendly adults for a night or two.

**1** We've chosen it to demonstrate the principle of pitching tents on a plastic sheet to keep them clean. Roll out a sheet of polythene bigger than the tent. Peg the four corners to keep it in position and then peg the tent out on top.

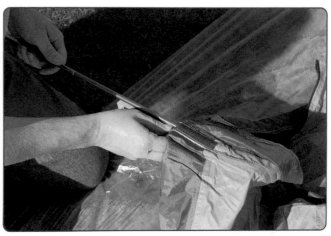

**3** Insert them into their sleeves – the sleeves are very small and tight and are sealed with Velcro.

**2** Unfold the simple aluminium poles. There are two sections, one at each end of the tent.

**4** Now the tent is taking shape...

**5** ... and can be pegged out properly.

**6** Trim round the polythene, keeping close to the tent sides. Excess plastic sheeting here can be slippery when wet.

**7** Job done! And however wet and muddy it gets, when you strike camp the tent will be clean and easy to pack.

## Getting ready for the season

Hopefully you'll have put your tent and other camping gear away clean and dry at the end of the camping season. Now spring is here and you'll be getting out your kit ready for the first outing of the year.

Here's a useful checklist:

- ■ Unfold and lay out your tent. Does it need cleaning? Are there any problems?
- ■ Check all the seams and fastenings and repair as necessary.
- ■ Consider if the tent needs reproofing.
- ■ Check the poles and replace or repair any that are bent or cracked. Wipe the poles over with a silicone furniture polish to prevent corrosion.
- ■ Spray the zips with silicone or rub with a candle or soft pencil lead (graphite) to ensure free running.
- ■ Check that stoves and lanterns are working properly. Stoves should burn with a clean blue flame.
- ■ Check the gas hoses to the cooker and replace if cracked or more than five years old (a manufacturer's date should be clearly printed on the hose).
- ■ Clean the kitchen equipment, sterilise any water containers, and use sodium bicarbonate solution on any cool boxes or refrigerators to prevent mould, odours, and bacteria.
- ■ Inspect all sleeping bags and liners. Clean and air them as necessary. Most sleeping bags and liners can be washed in a domestic washing machine, but check the labels before doing this.

# Large domes and tunnels

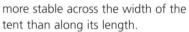

The vast majority of family tents sold today rely on a simple principle: the principle of the English longbow.

Look at the front hoop on this Outwell tunnel tent. A long flexible aluminium pole (the bow) is bent into a semi-circle and both ends are fitted into each end of a strong fabric strap (the bow string). The resultant 'D'-shaped frame is remarkably strong and stable because each part holds the other in tension.

Cross two or three of these 'D'-shaped frames at their centres and you have the basic structure for the frame of a dome tent. Stand two, three, or more up parallel and in a line and you have the skeleton of a tunnel just like the one pictured above.

These tunnels are easy to arrange to create a huge porch.

Or to have big opening doors on the side and ends to bring the outside inside.

The pole 'D' frames don't all have to be the same size. By varying these and adding tapered sloping ends, perhaps with a shaped porch area, to the tunnel a far more conventional shape can be created.

This example from Outwell shows exactly what happens and what a handsome tent can result. It could be a curvaceous dome, but in fact it's pure tunnel.

When you put up a tunnel tent each 'D' frame can be assembled on the ground. When all is ready they can all be stood up in a row, with the tent fabric and associated guy lines keeping them properly spaced and upright. This tends to mean they're far stronger and more stable across the width of the tent than along its length.

A number of makers have sought to cure this inherent weakness. Let's look again at our first picture. Outwell have linked the three 'D' frames of the main tent with a rigid longitudinal metal pole just above door level. Result: a much stronger and more stable tunnel tent.

Other makers have also found ways to link the 'D' frames together. Gelert,

for instance, use rigid longitudinal poles rather like Outwell; Vango create extra stability by using other flexible poles; and Jamet run a ridge pole along the length of the tent.

Extra poles and framework make for longer and more complicated pitching, of course, but there's always a price to be paid for technical developments.

Now let's look at domes. They use the same 'D' frame principle, the most basic designs crossing two or three of them at a centre point to create the familiar igloo shape. This worked quite

well in small sizes, but as such igloos grew in size two problems started to emerge.

First, stability was a real problem: large lengths of otherwise unsupported flexible pole could result in a tent that wobbled like a jelly. Actually, the tents were usually still strong enough to stay standing in the roughest weather, it was just that the wobble didn't inspire confidence. So the designers looked at other ways to cross the tunnel poles in order to get more stable structures. Tents like this Aztec were the result.

Four main poles, each in fact one of our 'D' structures, support each other to make that strong and stable skeleton tent designers are always looking for. You'll notice that other 'D' poles are added to give extra height and length at the ends.

Exactly the same idea worked in bigger and more complicated tents too. Look at this large dome from Vango. The skeleton is the same, but bigger and less easy to see.

The other way that large conventional dome tents could get rid of the wobble was by adding pods to the sides. This started with dome-shaped vis-à-vis tents and is dealt with in more detail on page 34.

Today tents like the large Sunnflair pictured above have a conventional dome for their centre section and add four wings or pods, in this case of tunnel construction. They offer stability to the basic tent as well as a lot more space.

The other drawback of big domes also needs to be mentioned. As we explained earlier, when putting up a tunnel you can assemble all the individual 'D' frames flat on the floor, but that's not the case with a big dome. Instead, putting a large dome up will involve you in threading a bendy wand perhaps 8m or 9m (over 30ft) long into

a sleeve on a huge and badly supported sail that you'll have to lift high in the air. No fun in any kind of wind.

This is perhaps the biggest drawback of the big dome tent. But looking at it from the bright side, your struggles will provide endless entertainment for your neighbours on the campsite.

## A warning about big tents

There is no doubt that family tents are getting bigger. For a few hundred pounds it's possible to get a huge tent, and these certainly appear to be a real bargain. Sadly, however, these really big tents are proving a serious problem for campsites and their owners. Some campsites have now banned them. Others often charge extra, or require a double pitch fee. One or two large holiday caravan parks have even stopped welcoming tents altogether, in order to avoid problems with oversize ones.

If you're thinking about buying one of these giants, think carefully.

Do you really need all that space? Do you have enough hands to put it up easily? And finally, will you be able to use it in all the places you want to?

# Putting up a dome tent

**1** Like most tents this dome tent from Coleman comes in a neat carrying bag.

**2** Lay out the basic tent. With this dome the inner tent is pitched first, and has a sewn-in groundsheet. As has already been advised (see page 24), this can be pitched on a thin polythene sheet to keep it clean and protect it from the mud.

Before spreading the groundsheet, check the pitch for sharp stones, twigs, or anything else that might puncture the groundsheet or damage the tent.

Take your time. Make sure the groundsheet is in the right position. You should always pitch your tent 'tail to wind' if possible – *ie* the door should face away from the wind direction.

Peg out the corners of the groundsheet whatever shape it is, and make sure it's stretched out to the correct shape with no creases or sections stretched too tightly.

**3** Now assemble the poles. One or more sections will be coloured and these should match the colour coding on the sleeves on the tent. Push the poles through the sleeves. Don't try to pull them – you'll simply pull the sections of pole apart. Generally it's a good principle to hold the fabric rather than the pole as you push it through and to centralise the pole so that the same amount is sticking out at each end of the sleeve.

**4** Now you can bend the poles into an arc and start to fit the ends into the bottom straps. This is much easier with two people, one at each end of the pole. With larger domes it's best to put someone inside the dome to lift the poles and the tent fabric whilst another person connects the poles to the straps at the bottom.

**5** There are two main kinds of fixing for flexible poles. The Coleman uses a nipple on the end of the pole that goes into an eyelet on the strapping fixed to the groundsheet. Just as common is a ring and pin, where the pin is inserted into the hollow end of the tent pole. There is little to choose between the two systems, although various manufacturers will try to convince you of the superiority of their chosen method.

With the four ends of the poles fixed the tent will start to adopt its dome shape.

**6** Now you need to fix the tent to the frame. Some tents use clips on an elastic tape, some use simple ribbon ties, and some use Velcro. These clips are only necessary if, as in this tent, the sleeves only cover the top third of the dome shape.

Fixed to the poles throughout their length, the tent has adopted its final full dome shape.

**7** Now it's time to unwrap the outer tent or flysheet. It needs to be draped over the tent, and this can be tricky, particularly if there's a strong breeze. It's always best to have two people to do this if possible.

Before you try fitting the flysheet ensure that it's the correct way round and that the doors, porches, etc, are in the right position to match the inner tent you've already erected. Consider any other special things that you need to do before putting on the outer tent. For instance, with this tent you need to put the pole that holds up the porch through its sleeve before lifting the flysheet over the inner tent.

**8** There will often be inner ties or clips and someone will need to get between the flysheet and the tent in order to tie or fix these.

**9** Now it's a question of finally pegging out the flysheet and the guy lines. Make sure the pegs are not straining door openings or, indeed, any other part of the tent. It's always a good idea to make sure tent pegs pull together both sides of an entrance or doorway, thereby taking the strain off zips or other fittings.

The basic principles demonstrated here apply to all tents with flexible poles, although individual makers will have slight variations on the methods shown.

# Putting up a tunnel tent

## Top tip

It's always much easier to erect a tent well if you know exactly what it's supposed to look like. Sadly, all too many tent instruction sheets are not illustrated. If that's the case try to find a picture of your tent in a brochure, or download it from a website before you set off.

When your tent is up have a good look at it. You won't be the first camper to have used the wrong pole in the wrong place and ended up with a tent that looks nothing like the designer intended.

**1** Although tunnel tents use the same 'D'-shaped frames, made up of a flexible pole and a strong strap, that are used in dome tents they use them in a different and much more controllable way.

When preparing a tunnel tent for erection you can assemble all the poles flat on the floor and then use the tent itself to pull them all up into position at the same time. This is particularly useful in breezy weather, when dome tents, particularly large ones, can seem to develop a mind of their own.

This medium-sized tunnel from Coleman is the kind that has different sizes of 'D' pole frames to give the tent a tapered shape. It also has a sewn-in groundsheet and inner tents that are permanently fitted into the outer tent and are erected with it. Not all tunnels are like this. Others have separate groundsheets and inners that are fitted once the outer tent is up.

Whatever kind of tent yours is you'll need to make sure all the doors, windows, and vents are zipped closed before you try to put it up. The best time to have done this is when you took the tent down the last time you used it.

**2** Lay out the tent where you intend it to go. Unlike a dome only the back end of the tent and groundsheet are pegged down at this stage. This rear end should be facing into the wind if at all possible and if the layout of the pitch allows.

The various-length poles are colour coded to ensure you get them in the right order along the tent. Thread all the poles through the correct external sleeves while the tent fabric is lying on the ground.

Never try to pull poles through sleeves. Thread them carefully into the sleeves, pushing and threading them through the tent fabric and moving the sleeve over the poles as much as possible. Don't force them if they snag. Equalise the poles in the sleeves, with as near as possible the same amount sticking out at either end.

**3** Once all the poles are threaded we can begin to fit the poles into the cross straps at the base of the tent. Start at the pegged-down end of the tent. The poles are each fitted to the end of the straps. This tent has a nipple at each end of the pole and these fit into eyelets in the straps.

Two people, one at each side of the tent and one on each end of the pole, certainly make this part of the job easier.

**4** As each pole is fitted into position it can be laid down, with its curve pointing towards the rear end of the tent and into the wind if there is one. Each flexible pole will overlap the ones already in place. Carry on along the tent until all the poles are fitted and are all lying on top of each other.

Now check that those initial pegs are still firm. It they fail to hold for the next stage you'll be top of the bill as campsite entertainers. When you're sure the pegs will hold, start to stretch the tent and groundsheet away from the pegged-down end. With a little help the row of pole frames will stand upright and the tent will start to take shape.

**6** When the tent is erect it can be held up with one or two of the main guy lines on the front of the tent. Make sure you peg them well. Then it's a case of going round the tent pegging out the groundsheet and the cross straps where the poles come down to the ground.

Step back occasionally to make sure everything is as it should be, with the tent adopting a smooth outline with no creases or stress lines. These are an indication that something is not quite right.

A bit of adjustment to pegs and guys will soon have everything shipshape and then, but only then, you can open up the doors, the windows, and the porch.

**5** Starting at the pegged-down end of the tunnel, make sure the first tunnel pole is in the correct position so that the tent fabric is taut but not too tight. Move to the next pole and again make sure that that section of the tent is adopting its correct shape and tension. Continue along the length of the tent, remembering as you go to check that each pole is upright, in line with the other poles, and parallel with them.

In some tunnel tents the design of the frame calls for some or all of the poles to slope. Even when this is the case they still need to be in line and parallel with each other.

## Linking those frames

We've already mentioned that a lack of rigidity is a weakness in some tunnel tent designs. This large tunnel from Khyam uses rigid steel poles to link the four main flexible poles that make up the basic tunnel structure.

The tent is erected in basically the same way as the other tunnel tent on this page. Then a telescopic steel pole, the full length of the tent, is added.

The ends of this steel pole fit into pockets at each end of the tent and Velcro tabs hold it along the length of the tent.

The telescopic pole can then be extended to tension the whole structure and is held at the desired length by means of a screw clamp.

# Putting up the new designs

**3** The big bag of steel poles will be familiar to anyone who has ever put up a frame tent. But hang on; is that a single bendy pole lurking in the bundle? Yes it is.

**1** Tents are changing and evolving all the time as new ideas and designs come and go. Though the best of them become popular and are quickly copied by other makers, most sink without trace, only to be replaced by the next revolutionary design that the makers hope will prove a great success and make them lots of money.

Here is the Sprint from Sunncamp, which could be called a new variation on the traditional frame tent. It owes a lot of inspiration to dome tents too, as well as to the garden gazebos that are also becoming popular as extra living space on today's campsites. We've included it because it incorporates features found in many other kinds of tent, as well as a few unique features.

No book can show you exactly how to put up each and every make and model of tent, but if you study the various step-by-step examples in *The Camping Manual* and get to understand the principles then you should be able to tackle any tent on the market, as well as some yet to be invented.

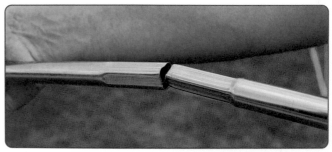

**4** The main roof poles are curved, so they need specially shaped spigots that can only be assembled one way in order to create the correct curve for the roof.

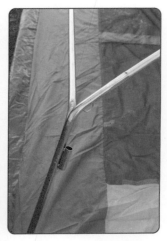

**2** Unlike most conventional frame tents the Sprint has an inner tent with sewn-in groundsheet. This is pegged out first.

**5** The frame is assembled over the pegged-out inner tent and the curved roof poles fit through sleeves in the canvas, just like a conventional dome tent.

**6** Look at this very special corner bracket that brings the various poles together at each corner. All frame tents have them, but not quite like this. As the frame is built the tent goes up.

**7** The sleeping compartment on the back of the tent uses that single flexible pole to give it its tunnel shape. A few extra pegs and the inner tent is up.

**8** Now the flysheet is draped over the inner tent and pegged out. Here it is nearly finished, with all the headroom and stability of a frame tent and the easy erection of a dome.

Will the Sprint be successful? Who knows. If it is it will certainly grow one or two more sleeping pods. If not, then there will certainly be other equally different tents vying for a place in the market.

**1** Here's another tent bristling with new ideas: the Vista Hybrid, again from Sunncamp. It's a dome-based design, but to get extra headroom across a greater floor area it uses rigid aluminium poles for the walls. These have curved tops to link with the flexible roof poles.

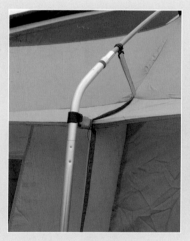

**3** Add the flysheet and the job is nearly done. Just the pegging out and guy lines to complete.

**2** With the inner tent up you can see the advantages of this design. All the headroom of a frame tent with the speed of erection of a dome.

**4** We hope this section has demonstrated that most tents, however new and exciting the marketing hype might claim, still use tried and tested principles. Understand those principles and new tent designs won't frighten you at all.

# Vis-à-vis tents

Some years ago if you wanted standing headroom you needed a frame tent or a tall dome. But frame tents tended to be heavy and take a long time to put up, while giant domes could be unstable. Indeed, some wobbled like a jelly.

Pyramid tents were popular, and easier to erect than normal square frame tents, and they offered a big floor area with useful standing headroom – but only in the centre. This example from Cabanon shows what we mean.

Then somebody realised that if you made the floor area a little bigger, big enough in fact to give two sleeping compartments as well as that centre section with the all-important standing headroom, you'd have a really useful type of tent.

This evolution happened in France, and as the two sleeping areas faced one another it soon got the name 'face to face', or *vis-à-vis* in French. The name and the style of tent stuck.

No wonder these vis-à-vis tents are so popular. Take a look inside this example from Sunnflair pictured above. The two sleeping pods offer comfort as well as a surprising degree of privacy for such a compact space.

Other designers realised that what would work with frame tents would also work with those large and sometimes wobbly domes. And there was a bonus: those sleeping pods added to each side made the whole structure much more stable.

Today vis-à-vis tents might be a dome or a tunnel or, like this welcoming looking Indus from Wynnster, use square, rigid pole, cabin-style frames for both the main structure and the end pods.

Designers who chose the dome style could even cross the dome poles somewhere other that at the centre of the dome, in the style of a small semi-geodesic tent, giving a more rigid structure. That's exactly what has been done in this colourful example from Trigano.

This vis-à-vis from Wynnster shows how tent designers can mix and match the basic shapes. Here we have a dome centre section with two tunnels as the sleeping pods.

Other combinations are possible, of course, and there's no reason why you need to limit the number of sleeping

pods to two. Three pods are common, and in fact the huge example from Khyam pictured below has no less than six. One is a useful porch. The rest can be used as bedrooms, or one could be a toilet and others simply for storage.

Altogether this tent is an amazing 8.6m (28ft) in diameter. You might find some campsites will want to charge you for more than one pitch if you arrive with a tent this big. Best sort it out with the warden face to face.

# A few ideas from across the Atlantic

All Americans seem to just love camping, and the tradition goes back a long way. The Plains Indians used, and indeed still use, the most distinctive shape of tent on the planet, which they call a lodge, or sometimes a tipi or tepee, or sometimes a wigwam. Tents were important to the Native Americans, so they had many names for their animal hide and tree-trunk homes, just as the Inuit or Eskimo peoples of the North had so many words for snow.

When the Europeans arrived they too brought tents, to provide shelter until they could build more permanent structures. In their great treks to open up the West they used what can surely be described as the ancestor of today's

**Above:** A selection of traditional tipis.

**Right:** This direct descendant of the tipi is available from Millets. It's a serious tent that will really delight children from seven to seventy.

trailer tents – the covered wagon.

Cowboys roamed the range, and what Hollywood Western would be complete without its scene around the campfire? No wonder camping is rooted so deep in the American soul.

Today many North American campgrounds offer traditional tipis as ready-erected accommodation for visitors. Full-size tipis are still being

made, not just in the USA but also here in Britain, and in Europe and Scandinavia. They're still manufactured using traditional materials as well as modern synthetics.

These large tipis and their direct descendants – such as the bell tents once used by the army and youth groups like the Scouts and the Boys' Brigade – fall beyond the coverage of *The Camping*

**Above:** The tipi meets high fashion in this model by Cath Kidston.

**Left:** This modern interpretation of the traditional tipi was made by Coleman for the Japanese market – the full story is on page 39.

**Below left:** Early models of this Cabanon pyramid were the origin of the vis-à-vis tents we deal with on page 34.

**Below right:** Other makes are still popular.

*Manual*, but smaller members of the same family certainly don't. Indeed, Millets sell a delightful 4.5m (14ft 6in) diameter tipi in their latest range. It's easy to put up. and its sewn-in groundsheet and details such as taped seams make it a real tent rather than a garden toy. It is available in plain brown or in a Cath Kidston cowboy print, and we reckon it will be a popular summer tent both at festivals and on family campsites. We also reckon it may annoy some more serious-minded campers!

The historical single-pole Itisa tent that we looked at on page 13 was also inspired by the shape of the tipi.

Tents of this shape are still popular today, and we tend to call them pyramids. The nice example illustrated below is from French frame tent specialist Cabanon. A steel frame and cotton canvas cover make it a sturdy weatherproof shelter. It was this shape – indeed, it may even have been an earlier version of this very model – that inspired the move to the shape we now call vis-à-vis, dealt with in greater depth on page 34.

Smaller versions of the pyramid are also made. A good example is this

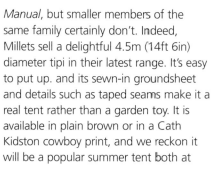

**Left:** American tent makers seem to prefer more rigid steel poles and the idea is gaining popularity this side of the pond.

**Below:** Another feature that has crossed the Atlantic are very large side openings on cabin tents.

**Bottom:** Today those trans-Atlantic styles have found a home in the best of European tunnel tents.

Peakland Challenger, sold through the Yeoman chain of shops.

Campers in the USA do, of course, use dome tents and tunnels just as we do in Europe. The tunnels that are popular over there, however, have one or two distinctive features that are only now gaining popularity on this side of the water. Rather than using flexible poles, for instance, they seem to prefer rigid poles in steel, aluminium, or a plastic composite, with straight side poles and gently curved top poles. This kind of tunnel offers better headroom over a greater width of the tent.

Here in Britain this shape of tunnel tent is becoming increasingly known as a cabin. Not all suppliers use that name, however, and – confusingly – many use the term tunnel to describe not only tents with these rigid angular pole shapes but also those with semi-circular flexible pole frames.

This tunnel from Vango shows the much squarer form of a true cabin.

The other distinctive feature of an American tunnel is its large openings. Our transatlantic friends do like to be out in the open air when they're out in the open air.

This handsome tent from Gelert shows exactly what we mean by a classic cabin tent – square in cross-section and with more doors than wall. That's a cabin.

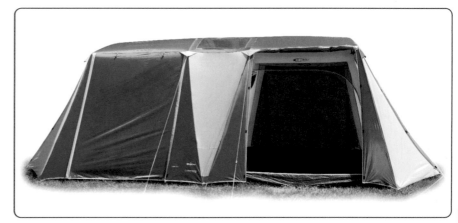

# Putting up a modern tipi

Here is one of the author's favourite and most used tents, the Coleman Hopi. An American design, it was for many years the best-selling tent in Japan. As well as being handsome, distinctive, and fun for kids, it is actually a very practical design. The Hopi is roomy, airy, and easy to pitch.

This particular tent has been well used for more than a decade in all sorts of places and weather. It has, however, been looked after. It is always put away bone dry, and is aired regularly, so it is still in great condition and giving good service. The nylon fabric and aluminium poles have many years' life left in them, proving that if you buy a decent tent and look after it, it will repay you with long and reliable service.

**4** The flysheet can now be lifted into place over the pole framework and pegged into position.

**1** Peg out the groundsheet. As with the majority of small tents, the groundsheet is sewn into the inner tent. This tent has the poles on the outside of the inner tent. Two long poles are fitted into the pins at each corner.

**2** The inner tent is hooked on to special fittings where the two long poles that reflect the traditional tipi poles cross.

**3** Four shaped shorter poles support the pair of long poles. With them in place there's a rigid framework to hold up the tent. Clips hold the inner tent close to the framework and give it its shape.

**5** . . . and perhaps best of all it's fun for campers from six to sixty.

# Family frame tents

**Above:** The French made Cabanon range of frame tents has models in all shapes and sizes.

**Right:** Even a medium size of frame tent can take up a good deal of space in you car boot.

**Below:** The frame of this kind of tent can be complicated. Most makers link the poles with springs but these can break or come undone. Always replace or repair them straightaway. It is also a great idea to mark the frame to show how it goes together. We explain how this can be done on page 50.

**Below right:** Most frame tents will have windows but not all. These two Trigano models show that this manufacturer offers both options.

Frame tents have been the mainstream of family camping for more than 50 years and they are still popular today. You just can't beat the average family frame tent for both room and, particularly, headroom, which reaches right to the edges of the roof. Frame tents can be very large indeed, but there's also a good range available in more manageable sizes.

When you're thinking about how big a frame tent to buy remember they're usually bigger and heavier than most other tents. They take up a lot of room and can be heavy to move about and load.

Like all tents, you can find a variety of qualities and prices when shopping for a frame tent.

Most still use steel frames (the gold colour in our picture is plating to stop

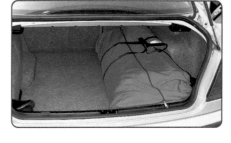

rust). Other manufacturers use painted or aluminium poles and some use composite poles, often known as fibreglass. Even plated or painted, steel poles can still rust, particularly if they get chipped, scratched, or damaged. Touch up the damage with either paint or varnish, because rust can stain the tent canvas and rust stains are usually there for life.

Different frame tents have different ways of dealing with groundsheets.

Most have none in the main tent but have fitted groundsheets in the individual interior tents. Check the strength of the groundsheet fabric and the depth of the turn-up at the sides. Some groundsheets zip into place.

You can fit individual rooms inside a frame tent, for sleeping or even, if you have small children, for use as an inside toilet.

Fitted wardrobes can be installed, giving hanging storage space for clothes and waterproofs.

Although we've told you that virtually all tents are now made in China there's one major exception: the long-established firm of Cabanon still makes all of its tents in Northern France. Cabanon's quality is second to none.

**Above:** This groundsheet from Cabanon has a generous turn up and zips into position when needed.

**Below:** This fabric wardrobe uses a simple metal frame and simply ties to the main tent frame for stability.

**Right**: Many frame tents come complete with colourful curtains and trim.

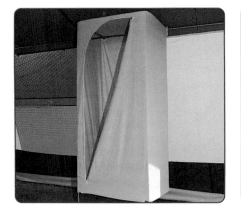

# Inside out or outside in?

As well as different shapes and different materials there's another important difference between various kinds of tents: do you pitch the inner or the outer first? Basically, the two variations mean you either pitch the inner tent first and then cover it with a flysheet, or pitch the outer first and then fit interior rooms.

Which is best? Campers have argued that one around the campfire long into the night. One advantage of tents that are pitched flysheet or outer tent first is that once this part is up you're out of the weather, out of the rain, and the rest of the tent erection can be done in comfort. However, this kind of tent often has groundsheets that are loose or only cover the bottom of the inner tent or tents.

Tents where you pitch the inner first will often have fitted groundsheets over the whole area of the tent floor, and these keep out dampness and – sometimes more important – all sorts of creepy-crawlies. They are, however, much more difficult to keep clean.

French tentmaker Cabanon, often the first with radical new ideas, have a fitted groundsheet that zips out for cleaning and zips back in to give you a guaranteed bugproof seal – top marks Cabanon!

As with so much in the world of camping, take advice, talk to other campers, and then make up your own mind.

# Top tip

Even sturdy frame tents can be damaged by weather. Tents are only temporary structures and a sudden squall or a howling gale can cause damage that's unlikely to be covered by the guarantee. Damage can also be caused by stray animals and plain run-of-the-mill accidents. It's therefore a good idea to think about insuring your tent.

The Camping and Caravanning Club has suitable policies, or your household insurer may be prepared to cover your tent. Other tent insurance specialists can be found in the pages of the camping press.

# Putting up a frame tent

There's no doubt that the sturdiest and most stable of the large family tents are the traditional frame tents that have been popular for half a century. These colourful 'bungalows', as they were then called, brightened up the campsites of the South of France and the Spanish Costas from the 1960s onwards and they're still popular today. They've withstood some incredible weather and family campers have learnt to trust them.

Some of that inherent stability, however, comes from their pure weight. The steel frames make their contribution, and the traditional cotton canvas covers still popular in this type of tent add kilograms too.

Let's take a look at a typical medium size family frame tent and how it's put up. We've chosen an example from the Sunncamp range.

**1** Bulk is showing already. There's a big bag of poles, and being steel it's a heavy bag. And in the other bag is the canvas cover, again pretty weighty. Finally, there's a bag of pegs and a mallet.

**2** Tip out the poles. They're linked with steel springs, and many have angled corner fittings for where they join one, two, or three other poles.

This Sunncamp numbers its poles with small sticky paper labels. They won't last, so follow our advice on page 50 and erect the frame so that you can number each corner using a small paintbrush and quick-drying enamel, to make sure putting the frame together is easy on future occasions.

**4** There are three short stubs that will fit in the front and hold up the porch. Don't put these in position yet but do ensure that the holes for them are all at the same end of the tent, the front. Now move round the tent inserting the legs, but leave the bottom joint 'broken'. Make sure the bottom half of the leg is pointing into the tent.

**5** Now unwrap the main tent fabric. Make sure all doors, windows, and ventilators are closed. Drape the canvas over the half-height frame. Be careful not to put too much stress on the frame – those poles can bend. You'll find it much easier to get the canvas onto the frame with two adults.

Watch that you don't snag the canvas on the corners of the frame. Plastic windows are particularly susceptible to scratching when you're doing this part of the job.

Take your time to get the corners to fit properly and tie the canvas lightly to the roof sections to stop it slipping.

One of the most important things is to get the porch fitted snugly. You'll find holes in the front of the tent to take the three short, stubby poles that hold the porch in shape. When the canvas is in position you can put these three poles into position in the pockets in the porch fabric.

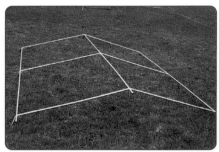

**3** Sort out the poles and familiarise yourself with what goes where. There's a frame that holds up the roof and eight legs. The legs are different lengths, but not by much, so you need to check carefully that you're getting the right legs in the right positions.

Assemble the roof section. It should look like the one in our picture.

**7** If you're doing the job on your own then a good tip is to always do one side first. The tent frame is much stronger on this axis and if you try to erect the front or back first it will put excessive strain on the front-to-back poles and they could be damaged.

**8** Do one side, then the other side, and finally the centre poles front and back. The tent will now be up but the legs will probably be sticking out at slightly different angels. Move round the tent adjusting each leg until it fits perfectly into the corner seam or centre section of the canvas.

**6** When you're happy that the canvas is in position and well fitted to the roof frame you can start to move round the tent putting each leg into its fully upright position. This is best done with two people, one erecting each leg of a facing pair.

Time spent doing this is never wasted. If you start pegging too soon you'll find you have to unpeg again to get the legs into position. When you're happy that the tent is the shape the designer intended, then you can start pegging out.

Start with the corners, and again make sure that the canvas seam is sticking close to the pole and pulling directly downwards in the same direction as the pole.

Today mudflaps on tents generally go inside. Tuck them in and get them to lay flat, to make an eventual seal with the groundsheets that you'll be adding later.

**9** With the edge of the tent neatly pegged down all round and guys in position you can open the door and move inside for the rest of the job.

All frame tents are different. This one has a small extension for a kitchen.

**10** Start pegging out the interior rooms. They'll nearly always have sewn-in groundsheets. Make sure the groundsheet of the inner tent lies over the mudflaps.

**11** Once the bottom of the inner tent is in position you can clip the top of it to the basic steel frame.

Make sure that the steel clips used face into the tent. If you fit them the other way round the sharp edges can chafe the outer canvas, and indeed can cause holes.

**12** Frame tent curtains use lightweight plastic mouldings as runners. These can be really fiddly to fix. Prize them open with a fingernail to get the process started. Don't give up – the system really does work once you've mastered its intricacies.

And there you are. A pretty view during the day and privacy behind your own curtains at night. The curtains have a ribbon across the bottom to keep them parallel against the sloping tent wall.

# Inflatables and instant tents

## Up in an instant

Tent designers all over the world are constantly looking for the perfect tent, the tent that will put itself up and provide a sturdy comfortable shelter with the absolute minimum of effort. Over the years there have been various attempts to find this Philosopher's Stone of the camping world. Many revolutionary tents have claimed to be just what every camper needs, only to subsequently disappear without trace. Here we look at a couple of the more successful attempts that are available on the market today.

The new Instant Tent from Gelert is the latest in a range of tents that really do erect themselves. A long coil-sprung frame is permanently fitted into the single fabric of a small two-berth tent. By twisting the frame the tent becomes a circular package, a little less than a metre in diameter and just a few centimetres thick. Unleash the spring – the most dramatic way is to throw the whole tent into the air – and the sprung frame turns the fabric bag into a remarkably elegant and practical shelter. As our step-by-step photos show, it's actually a good deal easier to do than to describe.

Karsten tents from Holland use inflatable tubes rather than conventional poles to support their main structure.

These tents are really only suitable for good weather conditions, but the Gelert Instant Tent would make a great shelter for a night or two at a festival or a summer weekend away for two friendly people.

Perhaps its best use, however, would be as your children's first-ever tent. They can put it up easily themselves, giving them amusement and something to do while you get on with the serious job of putting up the main family tent and, when that's done, having a quiet drink or a spot of relaxation.

## Held up by air

Despite the fact that they're quite rare, most people seem to have heard of inflatable tents. Indeed, many non-campers seem to be under the impression that all dome tents are held up by inflatable tubes rather than flexible poles. Perhaps this is because of the tremendous publicity that inflatable tents achieved by their tiny bit-part in the famous *Carry on Camping* film – but let's pass quickly on, avoiding pneumatic jokes at the expense of the film's star, Barbara Windsor.

Back in the 1960s the Pneumatic Tent Company borrowed the technology that was becoming popular for inflatable boats and replaced conventional tent poles with large-diameter rubber tubes. Today the technology is much more sophisticated, but the principle's exactly the same.

Karsten tents come from Holland. They're made from traditional high-quality cotton, and relatively small diameter tubes make up the basic frame of the tent. Some conventional poles are also used for doorways, porches and extensions.

Everything about these tents shouts quality. The fabric is heavy and long lasting, the zips are rugged and made for the job, and sizes are generous, and the prices reflect this.

Karsten have a particularly clever system whereby one or two tents erected close together can be linked by canvas connectors to create a much larger accommodation area. This is an exciting possibility, particularly for families with growing children. As the family gets older the kids can have their own tent but still safely joined to Mum and Dad's.

Another advantage of this system is that if you're travelling and stop for only one night you can just put up one of the tents, leaving the larger option until you arrive at your final holiday destination and set up camp for a week or so.

The other major inflatable range comes from Canada, the brand being AirZone. These tents tend to be smaller than the Karsten range and start with a two-berth model, the Goldfinch. AirZone tents have a rip-stop polyester inner and a nylon outer. Small diameter tubes are

# Step-by-step: instant tents

The packed instant tent is circular, slim, and easily carried.

Take off the straps, but hold the tent tight or it will try to unwrap itself.

Stand back and let the tent do its business. Or for a real spectacle, throw it into the air.

And that's it. The tent has erected itself and only needs pegging down.

inflated to a relatively high pressure (about 22psi), a safety valve ensuring that you can't over inflate them.

The AirZone comes complete with its own electric compressor, which will plug into your car socket to blow up the tubes. Of course, as with all inflatable tents you can also use a foot- or hand-pump and get some valuable exercise!

Both of the brands we've mentioned offer good quality tents, but at a price. Inflatable tents have always been expensive, as well as surprisingly heavy. Another disadvantage is that they can sometimes have a curiously rubbery smell that puts some people off.

However, when you see an inflatable tent turn up on site, watch the proud owner simply peg out the corners,

switch the compressor on, and sit back to watch the tent erect itself in just a few minutes. Then you'll understand the attraction of inflatables.

**Above left:** This Air-Zone tent uses high pressure tubes rather than conventional flexible poles. First the inner tent is inflated with an electric pump…

**Above right:** … then the flysheet is added.

**Right:** The inflatable poles of the AirZone have metal D-rings to fix to the base of the tent.

**Right bottom:** . . . and a safety valve to prevent damage from over inflation.

# The Khyam system

Perhaps the best-known and longest-established instant tents are those from Khyam. This large range of tents has been on the market for more than a decade. The system is based on a simple sprung 'knuckle' or elbow joint that can either hold a flexible pole straight or be 'broken' to let the pole bend.

The tent skeleton is permanently fitted to the fabric and putting the tent up is a simple matter of getting it out of it's bag and letting the poles fall into the right position. Working round the tent, the poles are straightened using the Khyam elbow joints to enable the tent to adopt its final shape. This is much easier to see in the series of step-by-step pictures than it is to describe in words.

Khyam tents come in a variety of sizes, and with some of the larger ones the poles can seem a little flexible. However, in their smaller sizes Khyams are excellent, stable dome tents that really are a doddle to erect.

Other manufacturers have now adopted similar designs and you'll find instant tents with other branding, but Khyam are still the best known and you'll see examples on campsites wherever you go.

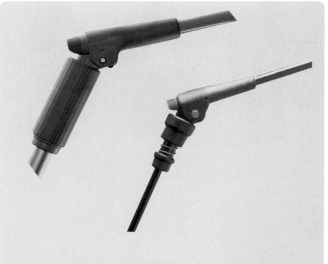

These are the knee or elbow joints that make the Khyam system possible. Different size tents have different weights of joint.

**1** Everything comes in a single bag.

**2** Once unpacked the poles fall into shape.

**3** Start to straighten the elbows…

**4** …and the tent grows.

**6** More sleeping room can be added.

**5** And this one has standing headroom.

**7** Quite a big tent.

**8** The porch is held up by conventional poles.

# Tent fabrics

## What will your tent be made of?

At one time tents were simple. They were all made of canvas, a traditional cotton fabric that starts off being porous but can be treated to repel water. Cotton canvas can rot, but once again, it can be treated to avoid rotting and to discourage mildew (that's the dark staining you get when you put away a tent without drying it properly).

Because the fibres in cotton absorb water, the fabric weighs more when wet than when dry. Cotton tents also shrink when wet, and when they're first used they'll let in a little water until the fabric swells to make the tent really waterproof (see the panel below).

Cotton fabrics can be coarse but can also be surprisingly fine, and the best fine cotton fabrics are without doubt the best material for making superior tents, even with their limitations. The Rolls Royce of tent canvases is Ten Cate, the brand name for an acrylic-coated cotton fabric. French manufacturers such as Cabanon use it, as do most of the best trailer tent manufacturers.

The drawbacks and the cost of cotton – particularly the need to look after it carefully if it's to have a long life and do its job of keeping out the weather – have led tent designers to look for alternative fabrics. Just as with shirts, 100 per cent cotton tents have been replaced by tents made from a mixture known as polycotton, consisting of natural cotton blended with polyester to produce a lighter fabric with the same strength as cotton. Just like cotton, polycotton can be used uncoated but is more usually treated to make it water-repellent. However, it can be difficult to make it fire retardant.

A common fabric for tents today is Polyester, which comes with a large variety of different coatings. A perfect coating is one that keeps rain out but

**Above:** A stylish modern shape but traditional cotton fabric. This is Ten Cate from Cabanon.

lets water vapour through. Such materials are described as 'breathable', and they make life far more comfortable, with less likelihood of condensation. Many manufacturers offer their own coatings under many different names. Sadly you are more likely to find breathable fabrics in outdoor clothing rather than tents..

Small or light tents will often be made of nylon, a polyamide that originated as a by-product of the coal industry. Individual nylon fibres do not absorb water and generally this means that nylon fabric can be made much lighter than cotton or polycotton canvases. Interestingly, you'll find that not only are the cheapest and simplest tents made from nylon but also the most expensive tents, destined for vigorous expedition use. The difference is in the coatings and the way the fabric is used.

Although untreated nylon can be used for tents, often because it is a fabric that breathes, it is usually coated to provide protection against water penetration. The coating may be acrylic, polyurethane (PU), or silicone. The quality and durability of these coatings varies, and as with most things in life, the better coatings are the more expensive. Acrylic is usually cheapest and silicone offers the best protection, although one drawback with silicone coatings is the difficulty in making them flame retardant.

Often the fine weave of a nylon tent

## Campaign for Real Tents

Many people, including your author, still consider cotton canvas the best fabric for real tents. It's natural and it breathes. It's the difference between wearing a pure cotton shirt and a nylon one. True, like Real Ale cotton canvas is an acquired taste and, also like Real Ale, it needs a bit more looking after than modern synthetics. But lots of us think it's worth the effort.

One oddity of cotton canvas can catch out the innocent beginner. Brand new cotton tents will usually leak! Sounds drastic, doesn't it? But it isn't really. New cotton canvas tents simply need to undergo a process called weathering. It's simple. Put the tent up when rain is forecast and wait for the clouds to open. The tent will get wet, some drips will come through, and all the cotton fibres in the weave will swell and nestle into each other.

The result? A natural perfectly waterproof tent, and one that will give years and years of good service if it's looked after.

Some tents will need two or three weatherings before every last drip is eliminated. Be patient: those last few drips will go, we promise. You can, of course, speed up the process and replace the rain with a hosepipe or a watering can, but don't bother. Just sign up for the Campaign for Real Rain!

material will be reinforced by a larger net pattern in the weave. This is 'Rip-stop', first developed for nylon parachutes, which – doubtless because of its early history – offers an amazingly strong, tear-proof fabric.

When a nylon tent gets damp the fabric slackens and you may need to tighten your guy lines to keep it in good shape. A more serious drawback with nylon tents is that the fabric is attacked by ultraviolet light, which means that strong sunlight can shorten the life of your tent. Modern coatings contain special light filters to reduce this effect as much as possible, but long exposure on bright summer days will still reduce the life of a nylon tent.

Another artificial fibre already referred to is polyester, and today you're much more likely to find a tent made of polyester than of nylon. This fabric is generally more durable than nylon but everything we've said about nylon pretty much applies to polyester tent fabrics too. Amongst the factors that make it perhaps the most popular tent fabric today are the fact that it doesn't shrink or get baggy when wet and that it is far less affected by sunlight.

Larger frame tents and many trailer tents are still made from cotton canvas but now have a heavy polyvinyl chloride (PVC) coating on the roof to make them strong and waterproof. The only drawbacks of this are the added weight and a slight tendency for condensation on the plastic-coated fabric.

Condensation can often be a problem with any coated fabric and that's why ventilation is so important in tents. Many newcomers to camping mistake condensation for a leaky tent, but if you buy a tent with good ventilators and use them correctly your tent will keep dry and comfortable.

## A tent on fire

No tent fabric is fireproof. Today most tentmakers claim their fabrics are fire retardant but all tents will burn, and some will burn remarkably quickly. That's the reason you should never use any equipment producing open flames inside a tent, and why – however romantic you think it may be – you should never *ever* use candles.

If your tent does catch fire there's only one thing to do: get everybody out and get clear of the tent as quickly as possible. Save yourself and worry about the tent later.

Regular tent-campers adopt an excellent habit – they all keep a fire-bucket full of water outside their tents.

Nothing is more effective if a tent does catch fire than half-a-dozen neighbours each throwing their own bucket of water on the blaze.

## Hydrostatic head?

Although we've tried to keep *The Camping Manual* as simple as possible, once you start looking at tents and the fabric they're made from you'll probably come across the phase 'hydrostatic head'. What does it mean?

Quite simply, it's a way of testing just how waterproof the fabric is. Imagine a piece of plastic water pipe. Stretched over the bottom is a piece of the tent fabric. As you fill the pipe with water the weight of the column will eventually push droplets through the fabric. Just how tall that column is – something between one and three metres, perhaps – gives you the hydrostatic head figure, and a way of comparing just how waterproof different tent fabrics are.

**Above:** Fire can destroy a tent in seconds. If your tent catches fire get everyone out as quickly as possible.

**Left:** A Bucket of water outside your tent is a good first line of defence against fire.

# Poles (and repairing them)

Tent poles used to grow on trees but today wood and bamboo have been almost totally replaced. Basically there are two kinds of tent poles: those designed to be rigid, and those designed to be flexible.

Frame tents and trailer tents will use rigid poles, usually of metal with angled joint fittings where they need to turn a corner or where a number of poles meet. Steel poles may be painted or plated to stop corrosion. Aluminium poles, less common in this size of tent, will be polished or anodised.

Frame tent poles will normally be fixed together, usually with steel springs, but these can come apart and you should always try to fix them back together before you put the tent away. It will make it much easier next time you want to put it up.

It's absolutely essential to mark the poles and joints of a frame so that the next time you put the tent up you'll know exactly where each part goes. Manufacturers sometimes have a go at this themselves, but not always very successfully. Some use paper labels that seem to come off the very first time a tent is put up and sometimes don't even survive the journey from factory to campsite.

Some people use tape to identify the pieces, but our suggestion is to use a fine paintbrush and one of those tiny tins of modellers' enamel in the brightest colour you can find. But make sure that it's quick-drying enamel, because you don't want to get paint on the canvas. Indeed, for this reason some experts recommend a bright nail varnish instead, but in our experience this chips off too easily – which is why we recommend paint; but do give it adequate time to dry before draping the canvas over the frame.

Put the frame up and check that everything is as it should be, then, starting from a convenient point, paint an identifying letter on every joint. If three poles enter an angled fitting, mark the ends of those poles and the fitting with a distinctive letter 'A'. The next fitting and poles will be 'B', and so on, until every joint is marked.

Even if straight poles are joined with springs or cords I'd still mark each joint with it's own letter. Then if anything goes wrong you'll still know exactly what goes where in the frame.

This job will take a fair time, but even if it takes an hour you'll save that hour over and over again putting up the tent on future occasions. It's an ideal job for a summer afternoon in the garden or even the local park when there's no pressure and plenty of time for the paint to dry.

Dome tents and tunnels will use bendy poles curved to form arcs. In cheaper tents these will be some kind of composite often known as fibreglass or glassfibre. Depending on the diameter and weight considerations they'll be either solid rod or tubular, and different methods of manufacture can result in a surprising range of strength-to-weight ratios.

One problem with bendy poles, especially in cheaper tents, is the risk of the pole snapping or splintering, particularly in cold conditions. Repairs are never satisfactory and it's a good idea to keep a spare section or two with your tent just in case. Sunncamp and some other manufacturers actually provide a spare pole section with each tent they sell, and Sunncamp have also introduced a new wrapped fibreglass pole guaranteed against breakage for five years.

Of course, they're not the only manufacturer to use wrapped poles. The idea of wrapped poles is that a layer of polyurethane or other plastic coats the outside of each pole and makes cracking or breakage less likely. Look out for name such as Durawrap or Durapole.

You'll find details of how to make temporary repairs to a pole on the page opposite.

A better alternative for flexible poles is metal. Almost always aluminium, or more accurately an aluminium alloy, these are light and strong and far less likely to break unless really abused. However, they can sometimes bend, particularly if trodden on. Try to avoid doing this, as although they can be straightened they'll never be quite as good or quite as straight again.

Whether bendy poles are made in fibreglass or aluminium, they should be linked with elastic cords to make assembly easier. If cords break repair them immediately. If you put a tent away with a few broken cords you'll experience utter confusion when you next try to put it up!

**Left:** Steel poles are strong but can be heavy.

**Above:** Complete replacement poles are available from camping shops.

**Below:** Modern flexible tent poles. These are glass reinforced plastic with metal joints

# Repairing a tent pole

Fibreglass poles are much more likely to crack and splinter than break completely. Any repair will result in a section that doesn't bend in the same way as the original pole. The repaired tent may consequently take on an odd shape, but it will provide shelter until a new pole section can be obtained. Bent or broken poles can never be repaired satisfactorily and the best option is to carry a spare section or two with you. However, if you do break or bend one here's the best way to make a temporary repair.

Buy as wide a reel of gaffer tape as you can find (available from DIY stores) and take it with you when you go camping, for as well as mending tent poles it provides ideal First Aid if your tent gets torn or your groundsheet develops a hole.

You'll be surprised how strong such a repair can be, but don't be tempted to treat it as a permanent job: replace the pole as soon as possible.

If you haven't come prepared with gaffer tape then insulating tape or even string can be bound round the pole in a spiral pattern. It's best to incorporate some kind of splint – a piece of wood perhaps. A tent peg is often suggested for this, but in our experience this simply doesn't work, because the hook at the end of the peg won't go through the tent pole sleeve.

## A more permanent pole repair

Some of the bigger DIY warehouses sell aluminium tubing in sizes that match common tent pole sizes. A piece of such tubing can be glued into position using a two-part epoxy adhesive.

This type of repair can be permanent, but once again the repaired pole may take on an odd shape in the tent. The repaired pole will be much stiffer than the original and certainly won't bend to the same curve. However, if you can't find a replacement for a particular tent it may be the only answer.

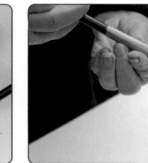

**1** Straighten the pole as best you can and try to tuck in all the splinters. Any that won't go back in tidily can be cut off. Be careful, glass fibre splinters can be very sharp and can cut or stab fingers all too easily.

**2** Small lengths of tape will help to tidy up the break ready for the main repair.

**3** Then cut a length of tape at least three times as long as the break – indeed, if practical as long as the pole itself.

**4** Lay the pole onto the long edge of your length of tape and roll the tape as tightly as possible around it. The easiest way to do this is to roll the pole across the tape using your fingers to ensure it sticks firmly all round. Add as many layers as are needed.

**5** Finally rub the tape tightly into the pole to allow it to bend into as smooth a curve as possible – it won't be perfect, but it will hold up the tent.

# Keeping your tent clean

Whatever your tent is made from, be it natural cotton or any of the synthetics, you should try to keep it clean and in as good condition as possible when using it.

It is possible to thoroughly clean a tent, but it's not a job anyone looks forward to. With thought and good practice you can keep your tent looking spic and span for a very long time without the need for major cleaning.

A really good idea is to use inexpensive builders' plastic sheeting under the tent. When it's pitched it will keep mud off the groundsheet and thus, ultimately, off the rest of the tent when you fold it up after use. Small sheets of the same plastic can be used for the same purpose around doors or wherever you're parking your muddy boots and wet packs and clothing.

Using plastic sheeting against mud is just one of several good habits to get into. Another is to keep all spare pegs, guys, and other small parts in a bag, and to wipe them off before you put them in. Keep the bag somewhere dry and handy so you can pop any bits into it straight away while camping.

Most dirt gets on to a tent when

**Below:** To keep your tent clean, cut off an appropriate length of cheap polythene sheeting. Peg out your tent and trim round the edges.

you're taking it down, particularly if it's wet and muddy. Really dirty tents are often the result of putting the tent away damp. The 'dirt' is in fact much more dangerous mould or mildew, which doesn't just make a tent look grubby but can actually render it useless.

To keep your tent in good condition and to avoid damage, always take it down in an organised way. Plan exactly what you're going to do and give careful thought to how best to keep mud off your tent in the process.

It's best to take down your tent when it's as dry as it can be, but that won't always be possible. We've all had to take tents down in the pouring rain but nobody does it unless they have to. Shake off as much water as possible and wipe the rest off with a clean dry cloth or a towel.

Now is also a good time to wipe off any mud splashes or bird droppings. If they're dry these marks will probably just brush off (use a dry nailbrush). If they need more elbow grease, use clean water applied with the same small brush. Only in dire cases use a little pure soap or a proprietary tent cleaner. *Never* use anything with detergent in it. Even the tiniest drop will ruin the proofing of your tent forever.

Once these little cleaning jobs have been done, empty the tent of

everything including the tent and pole bags. Put them on a small sheet of clean plastic and put the peg bag somewhere visible, so that everyone involved knows where it is and will therefore use it.

Unhook the inner tent or tents one at a time and neatly fold them on the hopefully clean groundsheet inside the tent. Put them away in their bags. Make sure you've removed all the pegs involved. Wipe these and put them in the peg bag.

It's very easy to miss a peg. You're likely to find it later when you tread on it barefooted or kneel on it. Ouch! Worst of all, you might snag the tent on it when you're folding up the canvas.

Now, one at a time, unhook all the main guy ropes. Roll up the guys neatly. Start with those guy-lines away from any wind. Take out each peg, wipe off any mud, and put it in the peg bag. As you remove further guy lines the outer tent or flysheet will collapse to the ground. Keep it out of the mud.

If you work to a system you'll find that nearly everything can be done under the cover of the flysheet and on that all-important clean plastic sheet.

If the tent is bone dry and well aired you can pack it into its bag. If it's even the slightest bit damp, or indeed really wet, you need another plan. If you have room in the car, drape the tent over the other luggage in the boot or perhaps over an empty back seat.

If you need to pack the tent away damp you can still do so, but it's absolutely essential that you unpack it and start the drying process immediately once you arrive home. Don't put the job off. Leaving a damp tent in its bag for just a few days too long has finished off more tents than anything else we know of.

Hang the tent up to dry, outside if you can or inside if you have room. When you're sure it's bone dry lightly fold it and put it in the airing cupboard. It will keep much better in there than tightly packed up in its bag.

# Reproofing your tent

An old tent leaking doesn't necessarily mean you have to start searching for a new one – which is a great relief, particularly if the problems start while you're on holiday. It's surprisingly cheap and easy to give your flysheet or outer tent a new lease of life using one of the many reproofing products available on the market, and you can probably reproof either the offending section or even the whole tent whilst on a campsite.

Do read the small print. Some products, for instance, are best used on damp fabrics. For others the tent will need to be bone dry. Some reproofing liquids come in aerosol forms and others need to be brushed on. For very large tents they can be applied with a simple garden sprayer.

If it's not an urgent repair then take the tent home and reproof it there, either in the garden on a bright day or even indoors, in a garage for instance. But if you do it indoors make sure there's plenty of ventilation. If you do this job outside, particularly on a campsite, protect the grass with a plastic sheet.

It is, of course, possible to find firms that specialise in reproofing if you don't fancy doing the job yourself.

Before you begin reproofing you must make sure that the tent is clean. We explain how this can be done on the page opposite. When you apply the reproofing fluid make sure that the plastic mudwall and windows are covered, since the fluid can make them brittle.

If you choose a coloured reproofer, not only will you give your tent a new lease of life but you might also improve its appearance.

To avoid a tidemark effect, treat each entire panel in one go if this is possible. Try not to overlap the layers – one coating should be adequate.

Finally, make sure your tent is absolutely dry before you fold it up to put it away.

**Above:** Always read the instructions carefully before starting work.

**Below and right:** An inexpensive paint kettle can be useful if you are reproofing with a brush.

## Top tips for waterproofing

- Make sure that you're not mistaking condensation for leaks.
- Sometimes just cleaning a tent may be enough to make it waterproof again.
- Never ever use detergent.
- Some cheaper tents come with unsealed seams and include a small tube of seam sealant. Although the job is really easy we advise only buying tents with pre-sealed or taped seams.
- Never use washing-up liquid to clean zips – it's good for zips, but it's a detergent and will migrate to your tent fabric and stop it being waterproof.

# Tent repairs: emergency and major

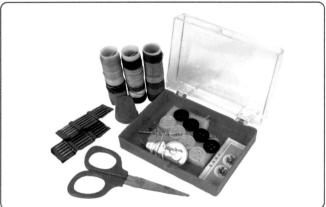

The most common damage and subsequent repair that you'll have to face with a modern tent is a broken or bent pole. You can find out how to fix them on page 51.

Almost as common are a split seam or a guy line anchor coming lose – it's all too easy to trip over a line or put just a little too much stress on to the seams of a small tent.

A small sewing kit that includes some strong thread will enable you to deal with most simple repairs of this type. The basic principle of neat and lasting needlework is to use small, even, and closely spaced stitches. Resist the

**Top left:** This simple kit will let you replace eyelets or insert new ones.

**Top right:** A simple sewing kit can handle small repairs to tents and other equipment.

**Below:** Seam sealer is easy to apply and will repair leaking seams.

temptation to hurry the job with fewer, bigger stitches. Take your time and you'll end up with a strong, neat job you can be proud of.

Most good tents will have tape-sealed seams. These can sometimes leak but are easy to repair with proprietary seam sealer (your tent may well come with a small tube). Don't try to seal seams until the tent is bone dry. Paint the sealer on to the seam and give it time to dry – a day or two is best, so do the job at the start of your weekend away. Sealer is sticky stuff and can adhere to other parts of the tent if you fold it up before it's dried properly. Never let seam sealer get anywhere near a zip.

Small tears, punctures, and rips in either tent fabric or groundsheets can be fixed temporarily with the same gaffer tape that we used for the pole

repair – another good reason to carry a roll with you when you're camping! Self-adhesive patches are available in assorted fabrics and colours and the better tents will contain a little piece of the actual tent fabric for more permanent patching.

The secret of a neat temporary repair, with either tape or a proper self-adhesive patch, is to make sure that the area round the tear or hole is clean and dry. Then get somebody inside the tent to hold a solid flat object (a chopping board or a book both work well) behind the hole so that you have something firm to push against. This will help you get the tape or patch to stick flat and firm, without creases or bubbles.

Finally give the patch and the area around it a good spray of reproofer. This should keep your tent waterproof for the rest of your holiday.

## Look after your zip

The zip fitted to your tent will probably serve you well, but only if you give it a bit of tender loving care.

Try to keep it clean. Wipe mud, grit, and dirt off as soon as possible with a clean damp cloth.

Zips should be treated with respect. Don't tread on them, and don't try to close one if the opening is too wide and will put the zip under a lot of strain.

Lubricate all zips occasionally. There are special lubricants for zips, such as Granger's Zipease; otherwise use a silicon spray, beeswax, or ordinary candle wax. Even pure soap will work until it gets washed off, but never, *ever* use detergent or anything containing detergent. It will lubricate the zip OK, but will migrate to the tent fabric and stop the proofing from keeping out the rain. You'll have a smooth-running zip but a leaky tent!

## An emergency repair kit for your tent

If you have the room, then there's a short list of useful items that will help if you have a problem with your tent – or, indeed, your other camping kit:

- Roll of gaffer tape.
- Spare pole section.
- Self-adhesive tent patches.
- Needle, thimble, and strong thread.
- Eyelet kit with punch and eyeleting tool.
- Spare guy lines and fittings.
- Tube of seam sealant.
- Aerosol reproofing spray.

You'll need to consider a more permanent repair, or perhaps a new tent, when you get home. If you decide it's worthwhile to permanently patch the tent yourself, here are some of the things you need to consider:

All but the heaviest canvas tents can be sewn with a domestic sewing machine, though you'll probably need a stronger, heavier needle. These are available from sewing machine specialists.

If you're repairing rip-stop nylon you need to be aware that the rip-stop threads in the fabric are remarkably tough, and can blunt and even break ordinary sewing machine needles.

You'll need to match both the thread and the fabric to the materials that your tent is made of. Specialist tent fabrics are not easy to find. Try your outdoor or camping dealer, or the original tentmaker or importer. Specialist dressmaking departments of large department stores might be able to find a suitable but un-proofed fabric that you can reproof after the repair is done.

Different threads are a little easier to come by, being obtainable from good traditional haberdashers – sadly now a dying breed – or from the sewing department of any large department store.

Another place to look for both fabric

and threads – and, indeed, pole materials – is in a specialist kite shop. Many of the materials and techniques used in kites are very similar to those used in the modern lightweight tent. Kite-makers know all about rip-stop nylon and may well be prepared to help out with patching or other small repairs, particularly in these very durable fabrics.

Once you, or someone more skilled, have sewn the patch you need to seal the seams with the proprietary seam sealer we've already talked about. Then use an aerosol of the appropriate reproofer to give the whole patch and surrounding area a good spray.

Zips can and do fail. That's why looking after and lubricating them is so important. If they do fail, replacing a small zip in a lightweight tent is not too difficult for somebody with some experience with a sewing machine.

Finding a replacement zip long enough for the job, however, might not be easy. The first places to try are your local camping dealer and the original tentmakers. Failing that, upholsterers or even the dressmaking departments of large stores may be able to supply a suitable zip. Some zips are sold by the metre with loose end fittings, but these aren't as strong as factory-finished zips if you can get one of the correct weight and length.

Don't give up too easily. A friend was about to throw away an old but otherwise well preserved heavily-built frame tent because the zip could no longer keep its huge door closed, and no suitable replacement zip could be found. But then someone suggested visiting a local caravan breaker, and there on a nail hung a huge bundle of heavy-duty second-hand zips, rescued from old caravan awnings. Among them was the perfect replacement. The frame tent is still giving good service!

With any repair, don't take on more than you're confident you can achieve. For more serious damage and jobs too big to tackle yourself you'll need professional help. Many camping shops

**Above:** An emergency patch can be applied more easily if someone inside the tent holds something flat against the tent fabric. With something to push against you can get all the bubbles and creases out.

**Below:** Once the emergency patch has been applied give it a good spray with proofer to keep out the water.

will either do repairs or, more likely, will know someone who does, and some tent manufactures will handle repairs on their own brands.

Try the classified advertisements in the camping magazines. They usually list repairers. Look in *Yellow Pages* for a local expert. As well as dedicated tent repairers look under the listings for caravan awning specialists, or, if you're near the coast, sail makers. Both have exactly the right skills and equipment to repair a large tent.

## Some tent repairers

At the back of this book we include is a far from complete list of professional firms who can help with major tent repairs. Some also offer tent-cleaning and reproofing services.

# Groundsheets and guy ropes

Builders' merchants and the big DIY warehouses sell rolls of polythene sheeting in various widths and thicknesses. You can buy it by the metre and it really is inexpensive.

Always pitch your tent on a base layer of this sheeting. The thinnest will be fine for smaller tents, while a heavier gauge will suit larger tents. It'll keep the bottom of the tent both dry and, more importantly, clean and free from mud. Indeed, when it's really muddy on site you can treat this basic groundsheet as disposable and deposit it and all its accumulated dirt in the campsite dustbins as you leave.

However, wet polythene can be very slippery, so do take care when walking on it, and don't be tempted to use it as the main flooring in your tent. For the same reason, trim the plastic sheet to match the exact ground area of your tent so that there are no potential slipping hazards around the edges.

Normally your tent, or the inner tent or tents, will have sewn-in groundsheets, as discussed in Part 1 of *The Camping Manual*. Camping stores also sell all kinds of separate groundsheets. Especially worth considering are the kind that let the light and air through to give the grass a chance to breathe. They aren't waterproof, of course, but are useful for porch areas or in awnings on trailer tents.

The other 'must have' is a travel or

**Above left:** Groundsheets come in many sizes and fabrics.

**Above:** This useful picnic rug has a waterproof back and has handy carrying handles when folded.

picnic rug with a waterproof backing. Used inside a tent it's like having the luxury of a fitted carpet, and outside on a bright day it's perfect for the great British picnic.

## Guy ropes

Modern guys are of synthetic cord, so they won't shrink or slacken as they get wet or dry. They fix to the main outer tent or flysheet via a metal or plastic ring, often with a rubber ring to act as a shock absorber. They always have an adjustment mechanism that allows you to set and keep them at the right tension. These can take various different forms and the main types are all illustrated here.

Sometimes the adjustment will be at the tent end of the guy, sometimes at the peg end, depending on which works best for a particular design.

Tent guys seem to be a magnet for feet. A good way of making them more visible is to

tie small brightly coloured ribbons or stick tags of reflective sticky tape on them. You can even buy brightly coloured or fluorescent guy lines, as well as some that glow in the dark!

Braided guy lines can sometimes fray. You can heat-seal the ends by touching them to a flame and then rolling them between your dampened thumb and fingers – but watch out, molten nylon can stick and burn.

# Tent pegs

**Left:** Wooden tent pegs are still available.

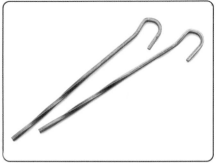

**Above:** Simple metal tent pegs.

**Left:** Colourful plastic pegs are easy to see so less likely to be lost. Plastic pegs are bulky and can break easily.

**Below:** This useful tool can extract most kind of pegs safely.

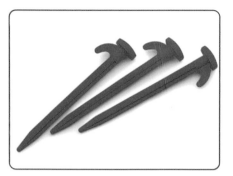

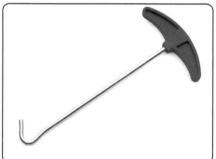

The basic tent peg might seem simple, but when you start to check out all the different types on sale at your local camping store you'll probably wonder quite where to start.

Steel pegs are the strongest, but also the heaviest. In addition pegs pressed from sheet steel can have sharp edges, and nasty cuts can result if you're not careful when pulling them out of the ground. Hardened steel pegs – like long masonry nails – are useful for rocky sites.

Plastic pegs are light, cheap, and easy to use and clean, but they can be bulky to pack and some kinds of plastic are fragile and can break easily.

Favourite are those made from light alloy, but hard ground or clumsy mallet work – or usually a combination of the two – can result in bent pegs.

Most campers will build up a collection of various kinds of pegs, because you'll find you need different styles of pegs for different purposes even in the same tent. Always have a few spares. However careful you are pegs always seem to go missing.

## Top tip

Always take a mallet with you when you go camping. It's always the best and often the only way to get pegs in. *Never* try to push them in with your foot. Pegs can and do pierce the strongest footwear, and your foot's next. This is a very common campsite accident – but you'll only do it once, we promise.

**Above:** A mallet of some kind is essential when knocking in pegs.
**Below:** Always ensure that your peg is in the ground at an angle of about 45 degrees so that the guy line pulls at right angles to the peg.

## Screw them in

The Screwfix system uses a rechargeable electric drill to actually screw tent pegs into the ground. The pegs come in two sizes but even the smaller ones are really too big for anything but larger tents or trailer tents.

The system is particularly popular with those suffering from arthritis or other hand problems that make using normal pegs and mallets difficult.

Screwfix pegs supply a special chuck adaptor and the rechargeable drill must have a torque clutch to avoid jarring if the peg hits a stone.

# Trailer tents and folding campers

**2**

In this section we look at trailer tents and folding campers. Some are small, simple, and quick to use. Others offer unbelievable luxury, as you'll see.

At the top end of the market they can cost as much as a car or caravan, but inexpensive units are also available. What they all offer is an accommodation unit that you tow behind your car (or in a few cases behind your motorbike).

They all have proper beds, and you sleep off the ground in all of them. Some need pegging out, while others can be unfolded and used without any pegging at all. These can be used on hard-standing as well as on grassy pitches.

# Why a trailer tent or folding camper?

There are many reasons to buy a trailer tent or folding camper. Perhaps your young family is growing fast and you need more space and somewhere for the kids to be inside on rainy days. Perhaps you're getting too old and stiff to put up a tent.

There's a wide choice of such units and this section of *The Camping Manual* takes you through them. First, the two main categories:

## Trailer tents

Generally, this term is applied to models where most of the walls are made of canvas. The tent fabric is folded out from the trailer and pegged out in the same way that you erect a frame tent. Indeed, on site it's often difficult to tell what you're looking at: is it a trailer tent or a frame tent? Sometimes the

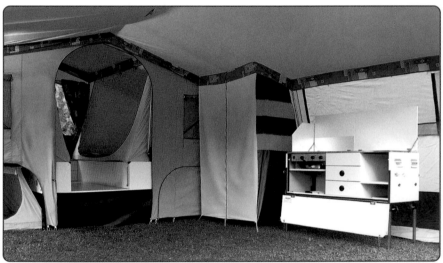

**Above right:** This simple flip top from Combi-camp is perhaps the simplest kind of trailer tent on the market.

**Right:** Inside the awning of this Conway you can see just what a small amount of the floor space is actually taken up by the trailer itself.

## Oversized and over here

Large folding campers have long been popular on the US market and over the years many have been imported into Britain. These rugged units last a long time so it's not unusual to find them on the second-hand market. Look for names such as Starcraft, Jayco, Bonair, and Coleman.

Some will have been imported by dealers who'll have made the necessary adjustments to make them road-legal in Britain, while others will be personal imports that may not have been modified.

Unusual chassis and braking arrangements, as well as American domestic equipment, can make spares and repairs difficult, but many enthusiasts are willing to accept that trade-off for the benefits of these large and luxurious transatlantic camping units.

Many of these American units have solid roofs with various winding mechanisms to open them up. Check these carefully, as repairs can be difficult and expensive, and always make sure the winding handle is still present.

**Above:** This huge American folding camper comes complete with a bath and two double beds – one of them Queen-size. Note the solid roof.

only clue is the tow bar protruding from the side of the tent.

Trailer tents offer off-the-ground beds that usually fold out from the main trailer body. A big advantage of them is that you can have an awning and sun awning covering more than double the space offered by the trailer tent itself.

Another kind of trailer tent is the flip-top trailer. In this case the trailer lid unfolds to become part of the floor of the camping unit, and canvas arranged like a giant pram hood unfolds to provide the weatherproof covering.

Flip-tops are amazingly quick to erect, often taking just a few minutes from arriving on site to being ready for use. The basic units rarely need pegging, although once again manufacturers offer awnings and sunshades which dramatically increase the amount of undercover camping space.

All awnings, sunshades, and similar additions are put up and pegged to the ground in the same way as conventional tents.

## Folding campers

Folding campers usually have a base unit that looks like the bottom half of a small caravan. On site the beds slide out to overhang the trailer at each end and a canvas cover protects it all from the weather. Because the entire tent is supported on the trailer, no pegging is necessary.

Just like trailer tents, however, many owners will use optional awnings to

increase the camping area, and these have conventional frames and are pegged in the same way as a large tent.

## Don't buy without a try

Large folding campers can cost thousands of pounds, so before you

**Above:** A trailer tent or folding camper can be fitted with a roof-rack to take bikes, small boats or other bulky loads.

**Below:** The Dandy Riva is unique among folding campers. It uses flexible plastic sheeting rather than conventional woven fabric for the tent covering.

# Trailer tent tips

**Above:** At a specialist trailer tent dealer you can find many different makes and models erected and you can compare them inside and out.

make the commitment you may want to find out if a particular unit suits you by hiring one. Some trailer tent dealers offer a hire service. You can find the

nearest hirer in *Yellow Pages*, the classified columns of the specialist camping press, or on the Internet.

When it comes to buying, whether new or second-hand, always get the dealer to erect the trailer tent or folding camper for you. Then get him to take it down and let you have a go. If the dealer isn't keen, find another dealer. You really do need to make sure you're happy putting the unit up and taking it down because you'll need to do that every time you take it camping.

## It doesn't have to be new

There are lots of second-hand trailer tents on the market. Here's a list of things to check out before you buy one.

■ Check the bodywork for rust, water leaks, or damage.
■ Check doors, lids, and catches for wear, and look at the main body hinges and frame poles, particularly where they fit on to the body of the tent.
■ Check tyres carefully. Make sure there are no bulges, splits, or cracking. It's best to do this with the wheels off – that way you can also check the wheel bearings.
■ Look at the canvas. If you spot mildew, walk away. Is there wear

## Saving space in store

Many trailer tents can be stored on their side. Manufacturers will supply skids or sometimes castors that make moving them relatively easy.

You'll need a couple of adults to tip them onto their side, but once tipped they take up a lot less room and can be stored beside your car in the garage, or perhaps against the wall of your house.

**Above:** Many trailer tents can be stored on their sides to save space. Some are fitted with castors or skids.

## Brakes or no brakes?

Small trailer tents will have no brakes whereas bigger units will. The law says that a trailer tent must be fitted with brakes if its loaded weight exceeds 750kg or the kerb weight of the car is less than twice the weight of the trailer.

Brakes will be fitted as standard on heavier models, and may well be available as an optional extra on small models. We would always recommend having them.

Another good piece of advice is never to tow a trailer which, when loaded, weighs more than 85 per cent of the kerb weight of your car.

where the canvas rubs on the frame or bodywork?
■ Check the seams for fraying and look out for water stains.
■ Are the zips working well?
■ Are the mudwalls in good condition? (Not all units have them.)
■ Windows should be clear. Look out for crazing, bad discoloration, or splits.
■ If there's a cooker, light the burners. You should be looking at a healthy blue flame.
■ Connect the trailer to your car and make sure the road lamps work properly.
■ While you're connected, make sure things like water pumps and interior lights work.
■ If there's a mains electricity installation, has it been certified by an electrician?

## Everything including the kitchen sink

Some trailer tents have a kitchen as standard, while others offer it as an extra. Some kitchens can be used without unfolding any part of the tent, enabling you to make a cup of tea if you stop for a break on your journey.

Trailer tent kitchens can be carried at the front of the unit, or at the back. Remember, either way a kitchen will add weight, so make sure it doesn't overload your towing ability. On site, once the tent has been erected the kitchen can be moved inside.

Some larger kitchens can take two adults to carry them. Kitchens often contain storage for gas cylinders, and removing these will make the unit lighter to carry.

## Watch out there's a thief about

If you want to keep your trailer tent or folding camper you'll need to think about security. They are easily transportable items, which means a thief can tow them away if you don't keep them locked up.

Most trailer tents will come with a simple lockable hitch, but usually these aren't strong or sophisticated enough to deter a real thief. What you need is a good hitch-lock, preferably to Sold Secure standard. (Sold Secure is a standards organisation that attack-tests anti-theft equipment. Items that have the Sold Secure logo will do their job well.)

Another good anti-theft device is a wheel-clamp. Sold Secure test wheel-clamps too, so you should again look out for their logo before you buy a product.

With a good hitch-lock and a wheel-clamp your trailer tent or folding camper should be safe enough against anything but the most determined thief.

**Above:** A rear end kitchen like this one fitted by Trigano can be used for a quick brew-up on a break in your journey.

**Right:** Fit a good wheel clamp to stop thieves towing away your folding camper.

## Here's one I made earlier

Trailer tents were invented back in the 1920s but they only reached their peak in the swinging '60s. Indeed, in 1968 there were no less than 26 makes of trailer tent on the British market. One came from Vickers, better known for building nuclear submarines! Barry Bucknell, the man who invented DIY, designed a plywood trailer tent that was marketed by the *Daily Mirror*.

**Do something worthwhile this winter**

For £137.14s. (or £30 deposit) you get the complete kit of parts with illustrated instructions written by the man who designed it, Barry Bucknell.

Our brochure shows how easy it is. To build (around 65 hours), to trail (even a mini will do), to set up (60 seconds), to store (5 ft. x 2 ft. of floor space).

Send for a copy to 'Mirror Tent Trailer'. Dept. C.O., Daily Mirror, 33 Holborn, London, E.C.1.

**Build yourself a Daily Mirror TENT TRAILER**

**Above:** A contemporary advert for the Mirror Trailer Tent.

# Putting up a simple trailer tent

## The Jametic

The Jametic is a simple easy-to-pitch small trailer that, when erected, produces a surprisingly spacious tent. In some ways it's a cross between a very simple flip-top and a conventional trailer tent but offering the space of a good-sized frame tent.

This set of step-by-step photographs will show you how to set up this interesting trailer tent and tell you a lot about other makes and models.

It's always a good idea to get the person selling you any trailer tent to show you exactly how it's put up. When they've shown you have a go yourself while they look on. It will make it much easier when you have to do it alone for the first time.

Take your time the first time you put up any tent. There's always a lot to learn. After doing it once or twice you'll be an expert.

We start with the Jametic unhitched, level, and on its pitch. We've taken off the cover and unhooked the kitchen unit. Now we can start the main business of unfolding and erecting the tent.

**1** Unfold the bed unit. Most conventional trailer tents will have a bed on both sides. This simple unit, however, has only one bed to unfold.

Mattress and bedding will usually be in place, but if we peep below we can see the secret of the Jametic's comfortable bed – sprung wooden slats. This bed could have come from Ikea!

**2** The bed unfolds to stand on metal legs. Don't put any weight on the bed until you're sure the legs are properly in position.

**3** Sprung steel poles form a frame that will tension the canvas. These frames are telescopic and have spring-loaded buttons that enable them to be extended to various settings.

**4** On this and most other trailer tents the canvas comes down to the ground and is pegged out as with a conventional frame tent. This particular unit has a larger tent than most, which covers quite a large area, much larger than the unfolded trailer.

**5** The framework needs to be adjusted as the tent is pegged out to make sure that the canvas is tight and tidy. Many trailer tents will need a separate awning to give much more tent space. Indeed, with most trailer tents the additional awning is bigger than the tent itself.

The kitchen that was unclipped from the back of the trailer now stands on its own legs beneath the awning. Connected to a gas bottle and provided with water it has all you need for preparing even the grandest meal.

**6** Inside, that comfortable bed is now in its own curtained compartment. Next door the original body of the tent provides seats for four and a freestanding table for eating or to relax around when the weather isn't conducive to sitting outside.

**7** An additional bed can be fitted to replace the seats and tables, and further fabric sleeping compartments or a toilet compartment can be hung from the main frame of the awning.

**8** No two trailer tents are the same, and the Jametic is just one of a large range available from long-established French tentmaker Andre Jamet. However, the principles shown on this page hold good for most trailer tents and individual variations will usually be self-evident, easily learnt, and simple to deal with.

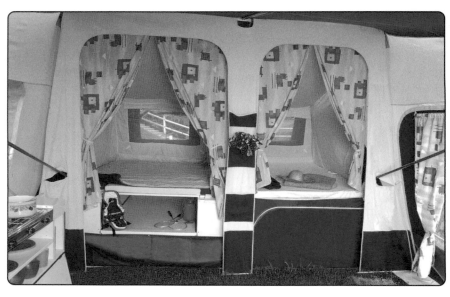

# Putting up a trailer tent

Let's look at how some pretty standard trailer tents are erected. We'll start with a simple unit from the Trigano Jamet range of French-built units.

First the trailer needs to be positioned on the pitch, and if the pitch isn't level you'll need to level the trailer as much as possible. A spirit level is very useful at this stage.

Trailer tents can have wind-down corner steadies or, as in this case, simple telescopic legs with screw clamps to hold them in position. These allow you to adjust the trailer to get it level both along and across the pitch. If the pitch has much of a slope across it you may need wooden boards or plastic chocks to get it level.

**1** Once you're happy with the positioning of the trailer you can take off the cover and start to unfold.

**2** With bedding in place and the canvas of the inner tent to be pulled into position this can be quite a heavy job. The legs of this unit act as extended handles and this is a great help, particularly if the assistance of a second adult isn't available.

**3** Watch out as the bed board gets to the vertical position. Suddenly that weight you were struggling to lift will be wanting to fall. Keep it under control and let it come down into position gently.

The cantilevered bed will have legs to support it. Adjust these so that the bed is level and there are no undue strains or stresses in the structure.

Once you're happy that all is well on the first side of the unit you can move to the other side.

**4** Though the procedure is almost the same the pull is actually slightly greater because you're also erecting the centre section of the roof.

Get the legs into position. Once again, check these to ensure that the bed is level and that there are no stresses or strains.

**5** Now you'll need to adjust the poles to tension the canvas. Different methods are used on different tents. You may find sprung buttons fitting into a series of spaced holes to adjust the telescopic poles. Threaded clamps are used on other makes and models, while some trailer tents use spring loaded telescopic frames that should give the correct positioning and tension automatically.

Whichever kind of adjustment your particular trailer tent uses, the principle is the same: you have to tension the canvas so that there are no creases or folds caused by excessive stress.

Before we look at erecting the outer tent let's look at that basic unfolding process for a trailer tent from another manufacturer.

This series of pictures are of a simple trailer tent from Raclet. The details are different, but as you can see, the principles are identical.

**b** Over goes the first bed. It is settled onto its legs.

**d** The pole framework is different but the principles are the same. Get the canvas tight but not over tight.

**a** Covers off and all is level.

**c** The other side is opened up.

**e** And there you are. Inner tent up and the outer cover neatly folded on the roof and ready to go.

Let's move on. Erecting the outer tent is simple but can take a little time. There are often lots of pegs to hammer in with this type of trailer tent. (Tent pegs are discussed more fully on page 57).

We've moved to a different tent but it's still a Raclet. Once the outer tent is unrolled it looks like a tent – indeed, it could almost be a conventional frame tent. Take your time pegging out. Remember the principle: tight, but not too tight. Avoid creases and stress lines, just as you did with the inner tent.

**6** Big creases or very tightly strained canvas are often a sign that something is wrong with either the poles that make up the frame, or sometimes the way the basic trailer has been pitched.

Always sort out what's wrong and put it right. Often just a small adjustment will sort everything out and you can move on.

The outer tent or flysheet will have been folded along each side of the roof when the tent was last put away.

**7** Now you can think about adding space with an awning. This will more than double the living space of a trailer tent. You can still sleep off the floor in the bedrooms that fold out of the trailer, but you can use the space in the awning for cooking, eating, more sleeping space, or just chilling out.

**8** Erecting the awning starts with assembling a jointed steel frame that's fitted to the front of the trailer tent structure. The process is very similar to erecting an ordinary frame tent, and we look at this in some detail on page 40. The frame is erected but with the legs 'broken' at the first joint exactly as when erecting a frame tent. The fabric is draped over the frame and fitted to the front of the trailer tent itself.

Then the legs can be stepped up and extended to their full length and the awning canvas can be pegged out.

# Sophisticated folding campers

Camping units don't come any more luxurious than this top-of-the-range Pennine Pathfinder. Pennine, a British firm, have been making folding campers in Lancashire for over 25 years so the quality is good and they've really sorted out the design.

This is a big unit. It weighs just on a tonne when fully loaded, so you'll need a decent-sized car to tow it (see the section on towing on page 72). Remember that with most tow cars you won't have any visibility over the top, so you'll need extension mirrors just as you would when, for instance, towing a caravan.

Standard equipment inside includes mains electrics so you can hook-up on site and enjoy most of the comforts of home. The kitchen has a gas stove with three burners plus an oven and grill. The stainless steel sink and drainer get hot and cold water from a pumped system that includes a built-in water heater. The kitchen also has a three-way fridge (mains, 12-volt , and gas).

To keep you warm there's a blown-air central heating system that works either on mains electricity when you have a hook-up on site or from bottled gas when you don't.

There are three double beds, one of them king-size. When you arrive on site two of the double beds slide out to overhang each end of the trailer. These two are proper beds with one-piece mattresses just like the ones you sleep on at home. It's good news not to have to

assemble them from seat cushions and seat backs as in the average caravan.

When the two beds are slid out of the way what you have is very much like a modern caravan. We've already looked at the kitchen. There's also a dedicated washroom with a fitted cassette toilet that even has an electric flush.

A proper wardrobe is fitted and there are plenty of cupboards and shelf units, giving lots of storage space. However, all of this furniture leads to what is perhaps the

**Above:** Real luxury under canvas. That's a folding camper.

**Below left:** Folded for the road, the Pennine is a large unit and with a normal tow car there will be little real visibility over the trailer.

**Below right:** Folding campers can be used overnight like this, but most owners will add an awning for more space.

main downside of this kind of unit: when you arrive on site it has to be unfolded and assembled before use. The systems are well worked out and pretty nifty, but you'll need practice at putting it all together, and even then it'll take a fair bit of time.

The double dinette offers comfortable seating but only for five, and that's a bit of a squeeze. So if there really are six of you living in the camper then one or two will end up sprawling on the beds, which is no hardship really – indeed, you might

find the kids arguing about who sprawls rather than sits.

At bedtime, if you need it the dinette converts into the third double bed, and this one *is* assembled from the cushions.

Although this is described as a six-berth folding camper and, indeed, will sleep six adults, they'd need to be very friendly. For four adults or a couple with two or three kids it would provide comfortable accommodation for any length of holiday – with a useful spare bed for friends to stay a night or two if they join you at camp.

One major bonus those two double beds provide is great lounging during the day – and there is always lounging to do on camping holidays. They also provide huge daytime storage areas for clothes and bedding.

It's often those two slide-out double beds and all that they offer that convinces people to buy a folding camper rather than a conventional caravan. That and the fact that in a folder you're still under canvas – still a proper camper, but with central heating!

**Above:** The Pennine awning more than doubles the camping accommodation.

**Below left:** A proper flushing toilet and hot running water, but it's still camping.

## Top tip

We've said it before, but it's worth saying it again: if you're thinking of buying any kind of folding camper or trailer tent, then make sure the person selling it shows you how to put it up. Then have a go yourself. Make sure you're happy with the amount of effort and the amount of time it takes – you'll be doing it a lot.

If the person selling it won't show you how it's done or won't let you have a go yourself, walk away and buy it from someone who will.

# Erecting a folding camper

## The Barrons Lifestyle

The Lifestyle folding camper is made exclusively for Barrons, a caravan and outdoor dealer with branches all around the UK. It's built for them by Comanche, a trailer tent builder based in Spain.

This set of step-by-step photographs will show you exactly how to set up a typical folding camper. Other makes and models are erected in basically similar ways. Always get the person selling you a folder to show you exactly how it's erected, and then have a go yourself under their expert guidance. That way when you have to do it yourself for the first time you'll have a head start.

Take it slowly the first time. There's a lot to remember, but you'll find you soon get the hang of it and the rest of the family will find their own ways of helping. After two or three outings you'll be an expert and the job will go much quicker and more smoothly.

When you arrive on site manoeuvre the folder on to the pitch. Don't be afraid to move the trailer by hand if you need to do so as to get it into the best possible position.

**1** Now make sure the handbrake is firmly on. Hopefully you'll have chosen a flat pitch but you're still unlikely to have the unit perfectly level. Use a spirit level to check both along and across the trailer.

The jockey wheel and corner steadies will allow small adjustments but corner steadies are exactly what the name suggests – steadies, not jacks. If you need a lot of adjustment use wooden boards or purpose-designed plastic chocks under either wheel to level the trailer.

Take off the cover. Fold it up and put it out of the way.

**2** Unlatch and slide out the first of the double beds. Normally the mattress and bedding will be in place – indeed, you can fold these units with the beds made up, which is ideal if you plan to arrive on site late at night.

**3** The bed will have additional supports, usually tubular steel braces that run between the end of the bed and the base of the trailer. Never put any weight on the beds until you're sure they're properly in position. Sliding out the end will start to erect the tent canvas, as the picture shows.

**4** The bed at the other end slides out in the same way. Now the canvas will start to look like a tent. The main canvas will be neatly folded on the roof (at least, it will be if you put it away properly last time). Don't tension the inside frames until you've rolled down the sides. If you do you'll find them very high, and for most people out of reach.

**5** Once the sides are down you can start to tension the inside poles. These steel frames are usually telescopic and have spring-loaded buttons that enable them to be extended to various pre-determined lengths. Don't over-tension them at first; you can always push them up another notch if you need to when the whole unit is pitched.

**6** Now the sides need to be fitted to the trailer base unit. This will normally be by elasticised loops that hook over fittings on the trailer and under the bed-boards.

On other trailer tents the sides fold right down to the ground and are pegged out as with a conventional frame tent.

**7** Now that the tent is weatherproof you can climb inside and get on with sorting out the interior furnishings, such as kitchens, folding wardrobes, and the like.

Modern folding campers, particularly top-of-the-range models, can have a remarkable amount of luxury furniture and fittings, and these can take a little while to unfold and arrange.

# Towing, the law, and security

To tow the kind of camping trailer, trailer tent, or folding camper we've described you'll generally only need a Category B driving licence – the one you need to drive an ordinary car. However, larger car and trailer combinations have more rigorous licence requirements, particularly for drivers who've passed their test since 1997.

You must hold or be covered by at least third party insurance for any

**Below:** Large trailer tents and folding campers may obscure your rearward vision when towing. If this is the case the law says you must fit towing mirrors. This kind simply clips on to your car's rear-view mirror.

**Below right:** This breakaway cable (the red one) is fitted correctly.

vehicle you take on the road. This includes trailers. Though most car policies provide third party cover for your trailer while it's attached to the insured vehicle not all do, so you need to check with your insurer and inform them that you'll be towing a trailer.

Additional insurance for such things as theft or accidental damage may be available as an extension to your existing car insurance policy, or as a separate policy insuring the trailer.

An excellent principle when towing is that the heavier your towing vehicle is compared to your trailer, the safer the combination will be. As has already been mentioned, most towing experts advise that the laden weight of a trailer should not exceed 85 per cent of the kerb weight of the towing vehicle. Generally with the kind of

trailers we're describing that shouldn't be difficult.

Your vehicle manufacturer will also have a recommended maximum weight that you can tow. You can usually find that information in your car handbook.

Some of the larger trailer tents, and particularly folding campers, will obscure your rear-view vision when towing. If this is the case you'll need to fit additional exterior mirrors to give you a view along both sides of your trailer. These mirrors mustn't project more than 200mm beyond the width of the towing vehicle or the towing trailer, whichever is the wider.

If your car was registered after August 1998 your tow bar must be of a type approved to 94/20/EC standards, and it is best if all towbars have a fitting

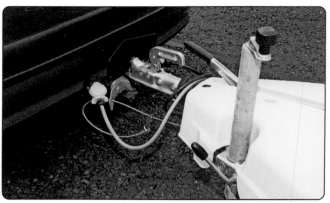

for attaching breakaway or secondary coupling cables.

Braked trailers will need a breakaway cable. This is a safety device that will apply the trailers brakes if it becomes disconnected from the towing vehicle. This cable is often misunderstood and confused with a secondary coupling. It's job is very simple: it's designed to apply the brakes and then snap, leaving the trailer detached from the car but with its brakes fully applied so that it comes to a rapid halt. The breakaway cable must always be in good condition and attached to the vehicle whenever you're towing.

Unbraked trailers have a different coupling. This secondary coupling is a strong cable or chain between the trailer and the towing vehicle. It's designed to prevent the trailer becoming detached if the main coupling should fail.

Tow bars will have electrical connections too. The car will usually be fitted with an international seven-pin socket, usually called the 12N, and this is connected to the vehicle's wiring system. Trailers have a corresponding seven-pin plug. Both should be wired to the appropriate international standard so that whatever trailer is connected to whatever vehicle the lights and indicators will always work correctly.

For some more sophisticated folding campers, a supplementary seven-pin socket called the 12S can be fitted to supply additional circuits for such things as interior lights, refrigerators, reversing lights, and battery charging.

A new international standard 13-pin socket has also been in existence for some time but has gained no real acceptance in the British market.

Unbraked trailers are restricted to a maximum total weight (including any load) of 750kg or half the kerb weight of the towing vehicle, whichever is less. Sometimes car manufacturers recommend a lower maximum total weight for an unbraked trailer. If such a recommendation is in place it must not be exceeded.

Most trailers will have a plate that gives the manufacturers' recommendation for the maximum gross weight. Do not exceed this weight – you'll be breaking the law if you do.

Another important consideration is the nose weight – that is, the weight that the trailer pushes down on the car's tow bar. It's important that this matches the recommendations of both the towing vehicle manufacturer and the company that made the trailer.

Trailers over 750kg or more than half the kerb weight of your towing vehicle must have brakes. If a trailer has brakes they *must* work, even if the trailer is small and light enough to qualify as an unbraked trailer.

EU regulations demand that:

- Brakes must be fitted to all road wheels.
- A parking brake must operate on at least two wheels.
- The coupling must be fitted with a hydraulic damper (unless the trailer was built before October 1982).
- Auto reversing brakes must be fitted (unless the trailer was built before April 1989).

Trailer tyres are covered by the same regulations as any other vehicle tyres. We give more details in the following sub-section.

Your trailer must have an approved number plate and it must carry the registration number of the towing vehicle. This number plate must be illuminated at night.

Your trailer should have the same lights to the rear as the towing vehicle.

Vehicles towing trailers have different speed limits to other vehicles. If you're towing a trailer you must not exceed 60mph on a motorway or dual carriageway or 50mph on a normal road unless a lower speed limit is indicated.

When you're towing on a three or more lane motorway you're not allowed to use the right-hand lane unless signs

**Above:** Special gauges will measure nose-weight accurately.

indicate you can or some lanes are blocked by road works.

Don't park your trailer on a road at night without lights, and remember that vehicles with trailers are not allowed to use parking meters.

Your trailer will have some kind of suspension. Traditionally trailers have used leaf springs, but today most have maintenance-free rubber suspension.

Trailer wheel bearings are a major source of breakdowns. Trailers can be overloaded, and they're often left unattended and unserviced for long periods. It's therefore hardly surprising that when they're eventually taken out on the road the bearings fail. Always have your trailer running gear serviced annually.

## Tyres

Trailer tyres must be correctly inflated, must have no cuts or other defects, and must have at least 1.6mm tread depth across the central three-quarters of the tread all round. It's not a legal requirement for your trailer to have a spare wheel, but if it does the tyre must conform to the same regulations.

Don't mix radial and cross-ply tyres on your trailer.

# Hitches and hitching

### *Hitching a trailer with brakes*

This is a typical trailer hitch as fitted to a braked trailer. The handbrake works in the same way as those in most cars. Press the button on the top of the handle to release the locking mechanism and pull the handle upwards to apply the brakes. On a pitch you may need to pull the handle into the completely upright position for complete braking.

The clamp in the foreground of the picture can take either a wind-down jockey wheel or, on lighter trailers, a simple tubular prop or leg.

Many people who tow, including the author, feel it's safer to take to the road with the jockey wheel or prop removed and stored in the boot of the car.

Lifting the hitch handle to about 45° will allow the hitch to be lowered on to the car's tow ball. Once the hitch is in place the handle will click into the down position, locking the tow ball into the hitch. A green collar on the red button will become visible to show that the hitch is locked on correctly.

If your coupling has no indicator button another way to test that it's securely connected is to try to lift the coupling, either by hand or, in heavier units, by winding it up on the jockey wheel leg. You should be able to lift

the rear of the car slightly, taking the weight off the car's suspension.

When you're happy that the trailer is safely hitched all that remains is to connect the breakaway cable and the electrical plug connections, check that all lights and indicators are working, and then you're ready for the road.

### *Hitching a trailer without brakes*

This is a typical trailer hitch as fitted to an unbraked trailer. There is no handbrake, of course.

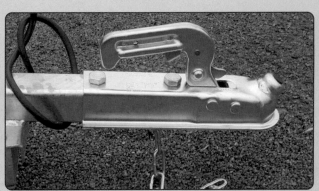

This hitch works in the same way as a braked version. Some hitches will have a red and green indicator button, others will not.

The hitch on an unbraked trailer must have a secondary coupling. In this case it's a sturdy chain, but it may also be a strong wire cable with a hook or loop at the end.

Whichever type of secondary coupling is fitted you must ensure that when towing it's hooked on to a pigtail or other strong point on the car's tow bar.

In this case too, once the trailer is correctly hitched and the secondary coupling is in place you'll need to connect the electrical plug or plugs and check that all the lights and indicators work properly.

# Safe loading (of car and trailer)

The importance of loading and matching of the towing vehicle and trailer weights as well as ensuring the nose weight on the tow-ball is within the recommended limits cannot be emphasised too strongly. These are the first and most fundamental steps towards safe towing.

### 1 CAR

The kerb weight of the tow car will be given in the vehicle's handbook. Your loaded trailer, if it has brakes, should never weigh more than 85 per cent of this weight, if it is unbraked it must weigh no more than 750Kg or half the car's weight, or the car's unbraked towing limit, whichever is less.

### 2 NOSE WEIGHT

Nose weight is the down thrust on the tow ball. Again your car handbook will have the recommended maximum figure for your car. Aim for about 7 per cent of the trailer's gross weight if possible but do not exceed the car or trailer limit.

### 3 TRAILER

The Maximum Gross Weight (MGW) is the unladen weight of the trailer plus the maximum weight of load that the trailer is designed to carry. You should never overload the trailer. If you are unsure just what your trailer weighs when fully loaded take it to a weighbridge. For safe towing your MGW should be 85 per cent or less of your car's kerb weight.

## Lights and indicators

All trailers must have the following lights, indicators, and triangles fitted to the rear:

- Two red sidelights.
- Two red stoplights that come on when you apply the brakes.
- Two amber indicators that flash at the same rate as those on the towing vehicle.
- A number plate light.
- Two triangular red reflectors to show that this is a trailer. (Today these triangles are often incorporated in a trailer's light cluster.)
- All trailer lights must be in working order. Trailers wider than 1300mm must have one or two fog lights unless they were built before 1979, in which case fog lights are not obligatory.
- There must be an indicator – either a light or a buzzer – so that the driver knows the trailer indicators are working.
- Finally, all lights must be visible when the trailer is in use. If your trailer has a rear opening this must not obscure any of the lights.

## Check your brakes

The safety of you and your family will depend on your trailer brakes being in good working order. Check them every time you hitch up the trailer.

Lubricate couplings and the brake mechanisms every three months or 2,000 miles.

Have the brakes, shoes, and linkages checked, reset, and adjusted every 3,000 miles.

When towing, feel the brake drums occasionally to see it they're getting hot. If they are, your brakes need adjusting. Any of the following warning signs can also indicate that your brakes need adjustment:

- Snatching or jerking during braking.
- Poor braking.
- No resistance to handbrake movement.

Other things to check include the rubber bellows on the draw bar. If it's damaged dirt can get in and damage the bearing surfaces.

## More information

Haynes publish two excellent manuals which give all the information you need regarding choosing, buying, and maintaining camping trailers. The information they provide is also very useful to the owners of trailer tents and folding campers.

*The Trailer Manual* by Brian Bate deals with all the things mentioned on these pages in far more detail than we have space for here.

Since much of the equipment is the same as that used for caravans, the owners of larger trailer tents and folding campers will find *The Caravan Manual* by John Wickersham packed with useful information, particularly for those who want to carry out their own repairs, maintenance, and servicing.

# Other equipment

# 3

Any Friday night at any campsite in Britain you see them arrive: car, or car and trailer, stuffed to the gills with everything including at least one kitchen sink. It's the living representation of the First Rule of Camping: 'Camping equipment will expand to fill the amount of space available to move it.'

Over the next few pages we'll look at sleeping bags and beds; stoves and pans; kitchens and fridges; water and waste; and, of course, toilets. We'll also look at clothing and all the other items you'll be tempted to *think* are essential for that camping weekend.

Do you need them all? Almost certainly not. If you had a smaller car, or no trailer, or if you had to carry everything on your back as many campers do, you'd still have enough kit to make yourself comfortable.

Somewhere between that and filling a large people carrier, a camping trailer, and a roof box and roof rack, is the point you should aim for as an average camping family: to have everything you really need, and space to pack it where it easily comes to hand where and when you want it.

Start the process by camping with the minimum equipment. Only buy a new bit of kit if you're sure you really need it.

It's far better to start with the minimum and observe how others do it on site. Talk to more experienced campers. Learn from their mistakes and from their successes.

# Sleeping mats and beds

A very few really hardy campers – perhaps the original friends of the earth – swear by sleeping directly on the ground. Most others would swear at it.

There are various methods of keeping yourself protected from the hard bumps of mother earth and, perhaps more importantly, from the cold and damp of the pitch.

**Above left:** This simple and inexpensive sleeping mat can still be comfortable.

**Above right:** A self-inflating sleeping mat. A simple way to get a good night's sleep.

**Below left:** A simple air bed. A good compromise between space and comfort.

**Below right:** A deep air bed can offer the same level of comfort as at home if you have room. Indeed this bed will double as a spare bed at home.

Simplest, least expensive, and taking up very little room, are basic sleeping mats made in various combinations of foam, and often from complicated sandwiches of different foams. The best of them can offer a remarkably comfortable place to sleep, belying their skimpy appearance. But don't be fooled, some sleeping mats are far from simple – high tech design in a very simple-looking product.

Next are the so-called self-inflating sleeping mats. Unroll them and their clever construction enables them to suck their own air in, usually leaving you no more to do than top up the pressure by simply blowing into a valve. Like their simpler relatives, these too can be remarkably sophisticated in construction and remarkably comfortable.

Next comes the conventional inflatable mattress. Although you can still buy simple blow-up beds consisting of a series of tubes, today's inflatable mattresses are likely to be far more sophisticated. The new generation of inflatable beds mimic in many ways the same choices you have when choosing a mattress for you bedroom at home. If, for instance, you and your partner are of considerably different build you can now get a double inflatable mattress with two sections that can be inflated to different pressures, offering both of you a comfortable night's sleep.

Mattresses come in different thicknesses, of course. Indeed, some of them will be as big and as high as your bed at home and offer comparable

levels of comfort. Look out too for thin cotton pads that not only add comfort but insulate you from the cold (and sometimes clammy) plastic exterior of your inflatable bed.

As always, however, there's a trade-off for the comfort of an inflatable mattress: they're heavy, and they take up a lot of room, both when folded and when inflated for use. But they *are* comfortable. If you're moving your camping equipment in a reasonable size of car and have a tent big enough to take it, then this is the type of bed to opt for.

Even lighter inflatable mattresses offer much more comfort these days. The internal structure could be a simple waffle design with walls dividing it up into separate linked air cells, or it may be far more high-tech, with plastic coils inside to make it as flat and firm as a good conventional mattress.

Other clever ideas include two single mattresses that can be zipped together to make a double or clipped together to make a double thickness single. You can even get an inflatable mattress with a hidden security compartment under a built in pillow to store valuables. This compartment will take wallets, passports, and cameras, and you can sleep in the certain knowledge that they'll still be there in the morning.

Of course, we shouldn't forget the traditional camp bed, comprising a strong canvas cover stretched tightly across a metal frame that lifts you off the ground. The taut canvas provides a

remarkably comfortable sleeping surface. However, although compact the frames are often of steel construction, and this can make them heavy.

Most family campers will opt for an inflatable bed, and getting the air into these is much simpler than it once was. There are still excellent hand and foot pumps, of course, but today a small electric blower can do the job using its own internal rechargeable power pack or conventional dry cell batteries. Some pumps will plug into the socket on your car dashboard, but for real luxury you can also find inflatable beds with their own built-in electric pump. However, you'll need to consider quality carefully here, because if the pump ceases to work the whole bed is useless. There's a lot to be said for a separate repairable or replaceable pump.

When buying your pump and bed, check that you can deflate it just as easily as pumping it up. It's actually quite a job getting all of the air out of an inflatable mattress, but with the right valves and a pump that sucks as well as blows the job becomes much less of a bind.

**Above:** A traditional camp-bed like this one from Yeoman can prove remarkably comfortable. This one has an aluminium frame to save weight.

**Below left:** This large capacity hand pump works well.

**Below right:** The lazy way. This 12 volt pump comes with all the attachments you need for any air bed or other inflatable items.

# Sleeping bags

**Left:** A warm sleeping bag promises a good night's sleep.

The key to a good night's sleep is being warm and comfortable. That normally means a sleeping bag, but not always.

If you're sleeping on a large inflatable double mattress in a tent with plenty of room you might want to bring sheets and a duvet from home and be really comfortable. After all, how many of us sleep in a sleeping bag at home? Campers who favour the duvet method have discovered that three duvets – one very thin, one medium, and one with a high winter tog value – can be used in all sorts of combinations to achieve exactly the right temperature. However, you'll need quite a lot of space, so the duvet system only really works for those who carry their camping gear in an estate car or have a commodious roof-box or even a trailer. It is, of course, perfect for trailer tents and folding campers where the bedding is left in place when the unit is folded.

Now let's look at sleeping bags proper. Most campers will tell you that after your tent the most important piece of kit to ensure camping comfort is the right sleeping bag. There are two real issues here, one of shape, and one of just what they're made of and stuffed with.

Simplest are rectangular bags. These come in various sizes, including some smaller ones for kids and even some clever adjustable ones that grow with your child. Two rectangular bags will often zip together to make a big double.

You'll find that some rectangular bags are fitted with a hood or cowl – a semi-circular addition to keep your head snug and away from drafts. Some will have a pocket in the cowl that can be stuffed with soft clothing to make a comfortable pillow.

From rectangular bags you move on

to tapered sleeping bags. There are also even more tailored shapes that take their form and name from Egyptian mummies.

Sleeping bags are made from various fabrics. The lining needs to be warm and comfortable – sleeping bags work, after all, by retaining your own heat, and need a warm body inside to function efficiently. On the outside you'll want a tough, fairly weatherproof coating, but one that breathes, so that it doesn't get clammy inside the bag. Between these two fabrics there'll be some sort of insulated filling that will normally be either synthetic fibres or natural down.

Down starts it's life growing on the breasts of arctic sea birds and if it can keep them warm it can certainly do the same for you. Geese, ducks, and the famous Eider are the best, but cheaper down may come from less thermal-efficient birds. Make sure you're not buying a sleeping bag stuffed with down from a humble pigeon.

As well as various qualities of down you'll also find down and feather mix, and just like pure down these too come in a range of different qualities. One important consideration with a down sleeping bag is allergies. If feather pillows make you wheezy you'll not get on with a sleeping bag with a natural down or feather filling!

The other big drawback with down is that it can become compressed into a solid mass, particularly if it's been allowed to get damp. Once down loses its inherent springiness, it's almost impossible to get it back.

For all of the above reasons, and on price grounds too, most people will choose synthetic insulation. This generally consists of polyester filaments that work in exactly the same way as natural down. They trap the air, which is what really keeps you warm. The biggest advantage of a synthetic bag is

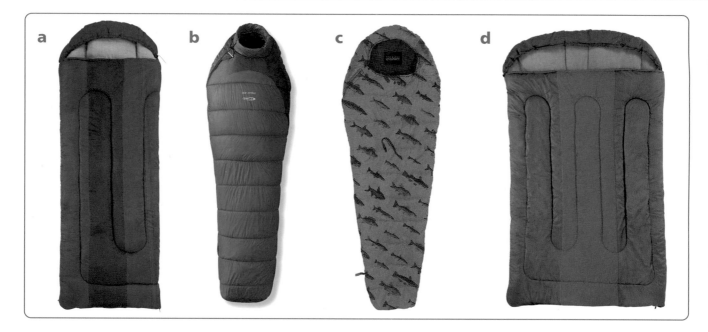

its resistance to damp. As mentioned above, if down gets damp it simply stops working. But a synthetic bag keeps some of its insulation even when wet, and if it does get damp it's far easier to dry out.

The main disadvantage of synthetic stuffing it that it takes up more room than a down bag. If space is important to you, however, you can get particularly compressible synthetic bag fillings.

You'll find lots of information on the labels of sleeping bags in a camping shop, of which the most important item is often the 'season' rating the bag carries:

■ 'One Season' indicates that the bag is suitable for summer camping in a climate no harsher than we usually experience in Britain.
■ 'Two Seasons' will also keep you comfortable in a normal spring and autumn.
■ 'Three Seasons' will keep you comfortable on most occasions excluding a hard winter.
■ 'Four Seasons' are suitable for all-year-round use.
■ Occasionally you'll find 'Five Seasons' bags that are really intended for

expedition use or at higher altitudes, amongst mountain snow for instance. Technical descriptions change over time and a newer classification system has recently been introduced, consisting of a European standard that gives actual temperatures in three ranges:

■ 'Comfort', the lowest temperature at which a normal person (in this part of the standard a woman) in a normal position will be comfortable and not cold using that sleeping bag.
■ 'Limit', the lowest temperature at which a normal person (in this case a man) in a rolled up body position will be comfortable and not cold using that sleeping bag.
■ 'Extreme', the lower extreme temperature at which there's a risk of hypothermia to a woman.

Bags using this classification will have three temperatures listed under 'comfort', 'limit', and 'extreme'. You also shouldn't forget that there are other factors that will affect your temperature and comfort that are nothing to do with the bag in which you're sleeping. These include whether you're a man or a woman, your age

**a** This rectangular bag has a simple hood.
**b** A mummy-shaped bag.
**c** Sleeping bags don't have to be boring as this example from Ted Baker at Blacks shows.
**d** A double bag from Coleman...

and weight, what you're wearing in bed, and even whether you've eaten recently and how tired you are.

The key thing is to find a sleeping bag that you like, that is comfortable, and that keeps you at the right temperature. Everyone is different and, as every couple have discovered as they fight for control of the duvet, no two bodies in bed get the same benefit from the same covering.

A word about zips. There's nothing worse than finding a cold metal zip in a nice warm sleeping bag. In most of today's bag designs the zips will be covered but it's still worth checking, and while you're checking make sure there's no tendency for the zip to catch the fabric – a surprisingly common fault. Coleman have recently introduced a special plough zip to avoid any such problem on their popular ranges of sleeping bags.

# How to stuff a stuff bag

When it comes to actually getting the sleeping bag into its container it's one of the rare occasions in life when neatness really counts against you. On no account try to fold the bag neatly to get it into the stuff bag. Just grasp the foot end and push it as far into the stuff bag as you can. At this point the job will seem impossible, but keep stuffing and amazingly the sleeping bag will eventually disappear into its container – almost like magic.

Some stuff bags will have extra webbing straps to compress the bag even more, but unless you really need to make the bag as small as possible don't go over the top, because in the long run too much compression is not good for your expensive sleeping bag.

An unpacked sleeping bag can be a large and unmanageable object. Trying to wrap it neatly can be a thankless task, but happily there's an easy solution – the stuff bag. Indeed, most good sleeping bags come packed in one.

Forget any notion of trying to fold or roll the bag neatly to get it into its container. Just follow these instructions and get stuffing:

Most modern sleeping bags travel in a stuff bag, a tough little container that enables them to be reduced to a minimum size for travelling. Stuff bags are really for travelling only, and if you want to keep your bag in the best of conditions you should take it out of the bag and shake it when you get it home then hang it up.

**1** It looks impossible – all that sleeping bag into such a small container!

**2** Grasp the foot end of the sleeping bag and push it in to the bottom of the stuff bag…

**3** …and keep stuffing it in.

**4** It *will* all go in, but only just. It will certainly fill the bag.

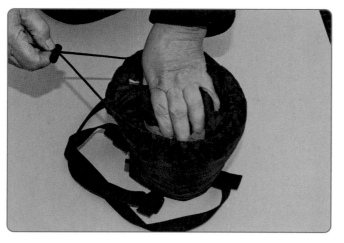

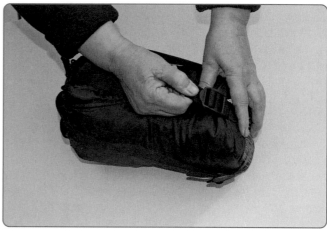

**5** Tighten the drawstring to close the bag and the job is almost done.

**6** On some bags additional straps can compress the package even more.

## Use a liner

Whatever kind of sleeping bag you choose you should give serious thought to using an easily washable sheet liner. These are available in various fabrics but the most popular is poly-cotton, for comfort as well as easy washing and drying.

It's perfectly possible to wash and dry most sleeping bags with domestic washing machines and dryers, but it's quite a big job, particularly the drying. Much better, then, to use a liner that can go in with the normal weekly wash.

# Stoves and pans

At home you'll generally cook with gas or electricity. The choice is wider when you go camping. Electric cooking is virtually unknown on campsites, although today some sensible campers are bringing electric toasters and even small electric grills with them. As with all electrical apparatus you'll need to make sure you don't overload the mains lead to your tent, or the campsite hook-up.

Today gas is by far the most popular fuel for camp cooking. It's clean, reasonably cheap, and once you know how to use it properly it's also relatively safe.

**Below:** A typical small solid fuel stove.

**Below right:** This stove burns Coleman fuel or unleaded petrol.

How big a stove do you need? Lightweight campers will often get by with a single-burner stove. Double-burners too are popular, but the author's favourite set-up is two single stoves: for a simple one-pan meal, or to boil a kettle, only one is used, but for a larger meal two can be used, making it a flexible and convenient way of cooking.

We'll deal with different fuels in more detail elsewhere in *The Camping Manual* but it's worth outlining here the various fuels your stove might use.

Some work with solid fuel. These are simple stoves, useful for warming a drink but not much good for serious cooking.

Liquid-fuelled stoves come in various kinds, but are often known by the generic name of Primus. Indeed, the Swedish company Primus still make superb stoves, not all of them liquid-fuelled. A liquid fuel stove can use petrol, paraffin, or even methylated spirits, the various advantages and disadvantages of which are dealt with on page 87.

Gas stoves are now far more popular than those using liquid fuels. Liquid petroleum gas (LPG) is available in various disposable containers, as well as refillable bottles or cylinders. It can be butane, propane, or sometimes a mixture of both. We go into more detail in the section on fuels on page 87.

Double-burner stoves will normally be run from a refillable gas cylinder, the most common variety of which is known to campers throughout the world as a Campinggaz bottle. These familiar blue football size objects can be found all over the world.

Larger cylinders are available and the best-known brand in Britain is without doubt Calor. If you have the room to carry it, a larger Calor bottle – or, indeed, any other make of refillable cylinder – can be used to fuel your gas equipment. You'll need a regulator, and different types of cylinder will require different types of regulator. You'll also need a length of special gas hose.

Coleman produce a popular two-burner stove fuelled by either lead-free petrol or a special liquid fuel known as Coleman Fuel (in fact just a very clean version of unleaded petrol), sold in small containers through camping outlets. These petrol stoves are very cheap to run, particularly if you buy your fuel at a petrol station, and once you're confident with them they provide a safe way to cook. They are perhaps the only serious alternative to the much more popular double-burner camping gas cooker.

You'll need pots, pans, and other utensils for cooking, whatever stove you choose. Many camping outlets sell versions specifically designed for outdoor cooking. Such camping equipment will generally be lighter and easier to pack than the kitchenware you use at home. However, it will often have foldaway or clip-on handles, and although the best of these can be very good indeed they can never be as reliable or safe as the fixed-handle saucepans you use at home.

Think carefully about this, for it's the dilemma of all camping equipment. The food you cook will be very similar to what you'd prepare at home, and quantities and meal sizes won't be smaller just because you're camping – usually quite the opposite. So do you really need smaller and lighter pots and pans? It's a fine balance. Clearly, if you're carrying your camping equipment on your back in a rucksack then weight and size are crucial. But if

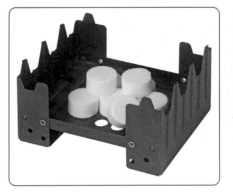

weight and size are not a problem – if you always go camping with your car, for instance – then there's a lot to be said for picking a pan that's good for cooking rather than good for carrying.

Increasingly, campers are turning to more exotic kinds of cooking equipment. One popular product is a large gas ring mounted on top of a refillable cylinder that has a number of alternative cooking surfaces. It comes with a flat or ribbed cast iron grill, often two-sided (one ribbed and one plain), ideal for grilling meat or fish or searing vegetables. The ribbed side gives those haute cuisine dark stripes so beloved by good steak chefs.

A paella pan is also popular. This is basically a large flat-bottomed frying pan, just as good for cooking bacon and eggs in the morning – particularly in large quantities – as it is for creating the Spanish rice and fish combination that gives it it's name.

A third option is a wok. Its curved bottom and sloping sides make it perfect for all kinds of stir-fries, and with the growing popularity of Chinese, Indian, and Thai dishes your own wok can bring the taste of Asia to the very door of your tent.

## An old favourite

The Trangia stove may have been invented more than half a century ago but it's still a popular choice for campers today. This storm-proof stove works just as well on a mountain-top as in the porch of a small tent on a British campsite.

Not so much a stove, more a complete cooking system, the Trangia can be obtained with different burner units. The basic burner uses methylated spirits, but gas and dual-fuel burners are available as accessories. Most kits include a saucepan, a frying pan, and a kettle.

Gas burners are available to replace the standard meths burner.

Today, the Trangia cooking outfit is obtainable in aluminium, in non-stick aluminium, or with pots made from an aluminium and steel sandwich for even more efficient cooking. The whole kit packs into its largest windshield for easy storage and transportation and takes up little room.

A dual-fuel version is also available.

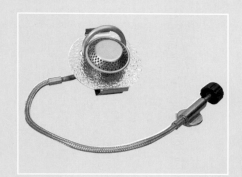

The basic Trangia cooking system has a stove, saucepan, frying pan, and kettle. This one has a meths burner.

# Lights, lamps, and lanterns

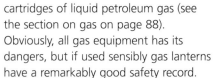

Every camper needs a good portable torch – absolutely essential to find your way back to the tent after an evening at the pub – and also a more powerful light to see what you're doing in and around your tent.

**Right:** A good torch is a key part of any camper's kit.

**Below left:** This fluorescent light takes dry cells or rechargeable batteries. Hung up in your tent it provides useful light.

**Below centre:** Small Gaz lanterns give a remarkable light.

**Below right:** A simple lantern that works on dry cells or rechargeable batteries.

The source of light back at the tent could be a small fluorescent fitting wired into your tent and powered by either a 12-volt leisure battery or from your car if it's on site and near your tent. However, most campers' choice of light will be a traditional lantern.

Lanterns come powered by a variety of fuels and in a large range of sizes and qualities. The most popular are gas lanterns, powered by small disposable

cartridges of liquid petroleum gas (see the section on gas on page 88). Obviously, all gas equipment has its dangers, but if used sensibly gas lanterns have a remarkably good safety record.

Liquid fuel lanterns are also available. The main brand here is Coleman, and the fuel is called Coleman Fuel, a very clean version of the same unleaded petrol you probably put in your car. If you buy Coleman Fuel in small cans in a camping shop you'll find it quite expensive, but if you fill up at the local petrol pump then a Coleman lantern is certainly the cheapest way of lighting your camp.

As you'd expect, some people are less than happy about filling lamps with petrol or storing petrol around their campsite, but liquid fuel lanterns can be safe products so long as you take the right precautions and adopt a sensible approach to using and storing the fuel – for instance, it's absolutely essential that you use a properly labelled, purpose-made can to move and store the petrol.

Electric lanterns are also available, of course. Today these mostly have a fluorescent bulb, giving a reasonable light, and an excellent battery life, whether they're running off conventional dry cells, rechargeable batteries, or an inbuilt rechargeable power pack. They're quick, easy, and absolutely safe to use, but sadly give nowhere near as much light as gas or liquid fuelled lanterns, and the cost of running them, if you're using ordinary dry cells, can be prohibitive.

# Gas and other fuels

Both lanterns and cooking stoves need some kind of fuel, and this chapter will deal with them all. But whichever fuel you're using you should always make your first consideration safety. Fires and naked flames are dangerous anywhere but nowhere more so than in a tent or around a campsite. When choosing your fuel, convenience and ease of use are important, but not as important as safety. Though most camping equipment is quite safe, it can only ever be as safe as the person using it.

Generally speaking there are three main types of fuel: solid, liquid, and gas.

## Solid fuel

Solid fuel camping stoves generally use small chemical tablets that are burnt in a tray beneath the pan support. However, solid fuel stoves aren't very efficient and you won't want to use one for any serious cooking, though they can be handy for warming a drink or a pre-prepared meal. Another disadvantage is that the fuel tablets can smell when burning and the fumes can upset some people badly. You'd be best to try them out before committing to this kind of cooking system.

As well as tablets, solid fuel can be supplied as a tube of paste. However, this has many of the same disadvantages as the tablet form.

Another solid fuel to consider is charcoal for barbecues, which we deal with on page 100.

## Liquid Fuels

### PARAFFIN

Paraffin has been in use for years and many traditional campers still find it efficient and safe. It's generally used in stoves that are pressurised and pump the paraffin through a pre-heater, where it turns to vapour that burns with a clean, hot flame. One major advantage is that this fierce pressurised

flame isn't easily blown out by a gusty wind.

However, paraffin is smelly, and if you spill it on your kit the odour will be with you pretty much forever. Make sure you store and transport it in proper sealed containers, and it may be a good idea to keep the containers in a polythene bag for extra peace of mind.

At one time paraffin was easy and cheap to obtain. It's still fairly cheap – perhaps the cheapest of camping stove fuels – but these days you'll need to seek it out. Try a garden centre, where it's still sold for use in greenhouse

heaters. Some of the larger DIY warehouses also sell paraffin.

### PETROL

In many ways similar to paraffin and used in similar stoves, though you won't normally need to pre-heat a petrol stove before lighting the main burner. However, it is far more volatile, and that volatility makes it far more dangerous, so that you'll have to be even more careful transporting and storing it. You also need to be aware that petrol fumes can present a real safety hazard.

With petrol prices constantly increasingly petrol stoves are getting more expensive to run. Unleaded fuel is best, but any fuel made for cars has additives that can block the very fine jets on camping stoves.

Most petrol stations are now hot on enforcing the regulations governing the sale of petrol into loose containers. You'll need to ensure that you have proper containers and that they bear the proper safety labels before they'll allow you to fill your can.

**Left:** A properly labelled purpose made fuel can is essential for buying and transporting petrol.

You'll find some lanterns and stoves branded as Dual Fuel. This means they'll run on both Coleman Fuel and unleaded petrol – indeed, some of the more sophisticated ones will use other volatile liquids as well.

### METHYLATED SPIRIT
This is denatured alcohol, and to stop you or anyone else from drinking it it's given a bright purple colour and a very unpleasant taste. Bought in builders' merchants or DIY warehouses, it comes at a reasonable price. Small bottles can also be obtained at High Street chemists, but at much higher prices. For some reason it's much more difficult to obtain in Scotland than elsewhere in the UK.

Methylated spirit burns with a clear, hot flame, but meths stoves are – usually – unpressurised, which means that they can be blown out by even a light breeze. Another danger is that in bright sunshine meths flames are virtually invisible, so never check if your stove has blown

### COLEMAN FUEL
This proprietary fuel comes from America's biggest supplier of liquid fuel stoves. Indeed, it's said that every GI in

**Above:** This stove burns Coleman fuel or unleaded petrol.

**Below:** Gas comes in a variety of refillable cylinders.

the US Army is issued with a Coleman stove that they keep for life.

These stoves use Coleman Fuel, but all this is, in fact, a refined version of unleaded petrol without the additives that might block the jets. Specialist camping shops sell it in small containers at prices a good bit higher than you'll pay for unleaded petrol at your local service station.

out by putting your fingers near the site of the flame.

Some people find the smell of burning meths unpleasant or worse. Unlike paraffin, however, meths spills evaporate quickly and generally leave only light staining or none at all.

### LIQUID PETROLEUM GAS

Often called simply 'gas' or, indeed, Gaz (although this is a proprietary name), LPG is a liquid contained under pressure that vaporises as it leaves the container to burn as a gas. Today, most camping stoves and non-electric lanterns are fuelled by LPG.

Two related gases make up most of the LPG market. Butane is perhaps the most common, but it has a minor disadvantage: it won't turn to vapour below 2°C. No problem for summer camping, but a disadvantage for more adventurous expedition campers.

The other gas, propane, needs to be stored at a much higher pressure than butane – about four times higher in fact. This means that containers have to be stronger and therefore usually heavier. Propane will easily vaporise down to –40°C, making it ideal for all-year-round use.

It's important from a safety point of view to realise that LPG is heavier than air, so a gas leak can lead to a puddle of gas on the floor of a tent that can

lead in turn to a real risk of explosion. Both butane and propane are in fact odourless, but the makers add a strong unpleasant smell so that leaks will be noticed.

Generally speaking most LPG appliances will work on either propane or butane, and increasingly you'll find a cocktail of the two gases is supplied, bringing the advantages of both to campers. Two-burner stoves and bigger will often use large, relatively heavy refillable cylinders. Calor is perhaps the best-known make: their butane cylinders are painted blue and their propane cylinders red.

The other way LPG is supplied is in disposable cartridges. These come in two main types, although there are numerous sizes and shapes. Pierceable cartridges are fitted to the appliance via a hollow spike that actually pierces the cartridge to let out the gas. Pierceable cartridges of different makes are interchangeable, but you need to check that they're made to European Standard EN417 Type 200.

Slightly more expensive but much better and safer are cartridges with an integral valve. These can be removed from the appliance when travelling, and the valve reseals the cartridge to retain the gas. The most common have screw fittings that comply with European Standard EN417 Type 2. Different sizes

Different refillable gas cylinders each need the appropriate regulator.

of cartridge are available to fit appliances of this type.

A few makers still produce their own unique cartridges and fittings. Some have clamps, some are screwed, and many claim all kinds of advantages, but you should remember that once you're tied in to any particular manufacturer's system you can only get refills from that particular maker and these may not be available everywhere.

Both pierceable and valve cartridges can be purchased filled with butane, propane, or a mixture of both.

## Gas safety

The most dangerous time with a gas stove is when you're changing the cartridge or cylinder. Make sure you're familiar with the way the cartridge fits on the appliance. Never change the fuel container inside your tent or inside a building – do it outside, and make sure there are no open flames about that might ignite any leaks. If you think the appliance is leaking, and particularly if liquid gas starts to spray out, get everyone away from it until the container is empty and the gas has dispersed naturally.

Dispose of empty gas cartridges with care. Never throw them on a fire – any gas residue inside could lead to an explosion.

# Changing cartridges and a mantle

## Pierceable cartridges

**1** Pierceable cartridges come from many manufacturers, but this one is by Campingaz, who invented the system. Once a pierce-able cartridge is fitted to an appliance it can't be removed until it's empty. These resealable cartridges are made to European Standard EN147 Type 200.

**2** Before you can unscrew the base of the lantern you need to press the safety lock button.

**3** The cartridge goes in the base.

**4** You'll need to press it down quite hard to locate it in the plastic lugs.

**5** As you screw the base back on to the lantern the connection on the appliance will pierce the cartridge and allow the gas to reach the control tap.

# The Campingaz Easy Clic system

**1** This system patented by Campingaz uses CV470 or CV270 cartridges. These are filled with a mixture of butane and propane. Always ensure the plastic seal is intact when you buy the cartridge.

**2** Check that the appliance is turned off. Push the Easy Clic handle into the open position and push the appliance on to the cartridge.

## Important safety notes

- ▪ Ensure appliances are turned off before fitting a new cartridge.
- ▪ Always fit cartridges outside, and never near open flames or cigarette smokers.
- ▪ If you suspect an appliance may be leaking, move it outside straight away and turn it off. When you check for the leak, use soapy water, *never* a flame.
- ▪ Always check the seals on the appliance. They should be seated correctly, in place, and undamaged.
- ▪ Try to move gas appliances such as lanterns gently when they're alight. If you splash the gas around it can cause flare-ups. If this happens, turn the appliance off and then let the liquid gas settle down.

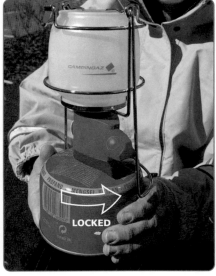

**3** Move the Easy Clic handle into the locked position. If you feel any resistance don't force it: make sure the appliance is seated properly on the cartridge.

**4** The Easy Clic handle in the open position.

**5** The Easy Clic handle in the locked position.

# Valve-operated screw fitting cartridges

**1** This simple screw fitting complies with European Standard EN417 Type 2. It allows an appliance to be removed from the cartridge, which has a self-sealing valve to retain the gas. Always ensure a seal is fitted and that it's in good condition.

**2** Simply screw the appliance onto the cartridge until it is hand tight. Never force it or use tools: you could damage the thread. Make sure the appliance is switched off.

**3** Switch on it's – as simple as that. Job done.

# Changing a mantle safely

**1** First unclip the handle from the lantern.

**2** Then open the heatshield.

**3** Remove the glass.

**4** This is where the mantle fits. Note the indentations at the top and bottom of the burner. The mantle clips into these grooves and is stretched across the burner to take up its proper shape.

**5** Take the mantle from its packet. At this stage it's just soft fabric.

**6** Put it over the burner, with the larger hole at the bottom.

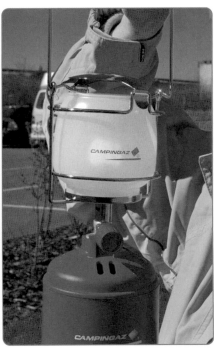

**7** Don't put the gas on yet, but light the mantle with a match or lighter. It will smoke a little, turn black, and then turn white.

**8** Now it's ready for use.

**9** Reassemble the lantern, turn on the gas, and light.

# Electricity: safety, mains, and 12-volt

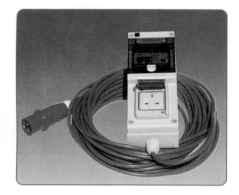

There are few subjects that prompt as much discussion amongst campers as electricity – particularly mains electricity. Most commercial and club campsites will offer electric hook-ups on some or all of their pitches, and although they're mostly aimed at caravanners or motor home users they're available to tempt tent and trailer tent campers.

Make no mistake about it: mains electricity can be dangerous. It can be dangerous at home and it can certainly be dangerous out in the open air. But so long as you use it the right way and take all the right precautions it can be used safely.

Pre-erected tents are hired out to beginners all over Europe, and all of them are wired for mains. Let's start by looking at how they do it.

They all use purpose-built electric leads specifically designed to bring electricity into a tent. At one end of the lead is a special weatherproof plug made to connect to the site's hook-up, and at

**Above left:** This cable is designed to bring mains electricity into your tent safely. It just has one 13amp socket.

**Above right:** Campsite hook ups use a special waterproof plug and socket.

**Right:** This electrical mains unit will clip onto the pole of a frame tent well above ground level.

**Far right:** This zipped opening will enable you to run an electric cable into your tent.

the other end is a special box with one, two or three damp-proof sockets to take ordinary 13 amp square-pin plugs just like the ones you use at home.

Wired into the circuit will be a safety mechanism known as a Residual Current Device (RCD). This is designed to cut the supply off immediately in the case of a leakage of current to earth. Such a leakage can occur when someone touches an appliance that's damp, particularly if the person is standing on damp ground – something which can easily happen in a tent.

These leads are available from camping shops and accessory suppliers. Do ensure the one you buy is made for camping. You can find similar equipment in DIY stores, made for powering garden tools such as

lawnmowers, hedge trimmers, etc, but these aren't really suitable for taking power into your tent.

Today's modern family tents will often have been designed to make bringing electricity inside much easier. To avoid cables across the doorway there'll be a small zipped flap where the cable can enter the tent. Ribbon ties will help you take the cable neatly up to the tent roof, and a sturdy hook will give you somewhere to locate the socket box well above damp grass level.

Some people will tell you that the campsite hook-up socket will already be protected, and although this is usually true it would be foolish to risk your own and your family's health and safety on that equipment.

The other important consideration is that even if you're using a purpose-made lead such as the one described above, it's important how you place it and the equipment plugged into it inside your tent. Tents, and particularly the floors of tents, can be damp, and moisture and electricity do not mix.

The socket end of the cable will usually have some means of fixing it well above level ground. Often special clips will enable it to be fixed to a frame tent pole high off the ground. Arranging to mount it off the ground in small dome tents is more difficult.

The equipment you plug in must also be placed safely: don't use electrical equipment on the tent floor.

Another thing you'll need to think about is just what equipment you can plug in. At home you'll probably have endless sockets and it's very hard to

overload them, but a campsite socket can be easily overloaded.

If you're using an electric kettle it really ought to be a small camping one. Heaters, too, should be small, ideally less than 1000 watts and designed for camp life. And don't try to run your heater and kettle together – you'll almost certainly overload your pitch socket, causing it to cut out. You may even cut out other sockets on the campsite!

The main reason people plug in is to watch television. Conventional televisions use a lot of power and battery-powered TVs don't get much viewing time on a set of dry cells or rechargeable batteries. However, new flat-screen televisions need a lot less power, and if you're buying a TV especially for camping they certainly deserve consideration.

## 12-VOLT ELECTRICITY

One alternative that's gaining popularity is connecting to the mains on site but running the wire into a transformer which immediately reduces the power to a much safer lower voltage. Exactly the same technology is used for garden lighting and some campers have adapted that equipment for use on site. However, everything we've said about dampness above applies to the transformer too. Make sure you mount it as high as possible and away from any moisture.

Some campers use the low voltage approach and plug their camping equipment into the car dashboard cigar lighter. Indeed, many cars are now fitted with one or more purpose-built 12-volt plugs. This system works well as long as

you don't sit up too late and use too much power, thus flattening your car battery. You'll be annoyed in the morning if the car doesn't start! To avoid this, some campers bring a separate 12-volt leisure battery with them, and it's possible to have a special charging socket built into your car for this purpose.

Remember, batteries are very heavy and contain acid, so make sure you have a way of firmly fixing yours in the boot of the car and be particularly careful when lifting or moving it.

## GENERATORS

Small petrol-powered generators are easily available today and for just a few hundred pounds you can bring your own power station – albeit a small one – to the door of your tent. However, all generators are noisy and there's no better way of annoying your fellow campers on a quiet summer's evening than to start up your generator so that you can watch *Coronation Street*. For that reason if no other many campsites ban generators or limit their use to certain hours of the day.

## SOLAR POWER

Solar power – or more accurately photo-voltaic power – is gaining in popularity among campers. Solar panels are available in all kinds of sizes. They simply take the sun's rays – indeed, any daylight – and turn it into electricity. A solar panel of the size most campers will carry won't run much equipment but it will charge a 12-volt battery and keep it charged on a long bright summer day.

## Top tip

Before you think about mains electricity, ask yourself: do you really need it? Gas or liquid fuel lanterns work really well. Gas-powered fridges are also excellent for camping. So unless you must take your television camping you probably don't need mains power, and real campers will tell you that getting away from TV is what camping is really all about.

Installation is easy. There are plenty of kits designed for camping use and the simplest can be connected to a battery via a lead and crocodile clips – but be careful of sparking. Other kits will require some simple wiring, and if you're not familiar with electrical equipment you may need to call an electrician.

Increasingly today you can buy camping equipment with small built-in solar chargers. Torches are available, which if left in bright light all day will light your way when darkness comes. Those little garden lamps with inbuilt solar panels make an ideal beacon to guide you back to your tent.

**Below left:** This transformer will reduce mains power down to 12-volts for safer use in your tent.

**Below centre:** Volvo fit 12 volt electric sockets between the front seats of their cars, ideal for using appliances on the back seats.

**Below:** This neat solar panel comes in its own carrying case and will help keep your leisure battery topped up on bright days.

# Cool boxes and fridges

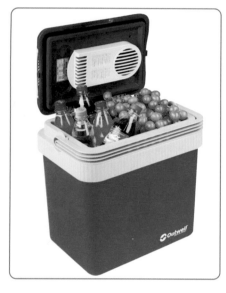

**Top:** Insulated cool boxes come in a range of sizes. For drinks insulated jugs are available.

**Above:** This Peltier 12 volt cool box can keep food cool but performance is not as good as with a proper fridge.

**Below:** This fridge runs on gas as well as 12 volt and mains electricity.

To keep food fresh and drinks at the right temperature you'll need some kind of cooler. Portable cool boxes and fridges come in a vast range of sizes and styles and at first you might be puzzled why some seem much more expensive than others. So let's have a look at what's available, starting with the cheapest.

First are insulated cool boxes. They have no cooling mechanism but you can fill them with ice or with special freezer-packs that you make cold in your freezer and then use to keep the contents of your box fresh and cold. If you pack your cool box with pre-cooled items from the freezer you'll usually find it's still plenty cold enough when you arrive on site. Many campsites will refreeze your freezer-packs overnight for a small charge, and with two sets you can keep your food and drinks nice and cool however long you're camping.

Next come small electric cool boxes. They use a device called a thermocouple invented by a French physicist in the nineteenth century: this is called the Peltier Effect after its inventor, and it's magic. Put 12 volts through the device one way and it cools down, reverse the current and it heats up, so you can use it as a cool box or bring home your Chinese meal piping hot in the same box.

You've guessed. There's a drawback. It only really works in small sizes, and it isn't as efficient as a real fridge. On a hot day, particularly if you're camping somewhere nice like the South of France, Monsieur Peltier won't be able to stop your butter going runny. For that you need a real fridge.

When it comes to real camping fridges the best of them work on two alternative kinds of power: electricity and bottled gas. Some will plug into the mains if you're on a campsite with electric hook-ups, and some will work from the 12-volt dashboard socket in your car. But remember that this only really works when the car engine is charging the battery. When you arrive on site you can connect them up to a gas cylinder. If you run the fridge from the car battery when parked or overnight you'll end up with a flat battery and a car that won't start.

You can even get a portable camping freezer. However, they need a lot of power, and do you really want to take a lot of frozen food with you when you're camping? On the other hand, if you combine your camping holidays with visits to pick-your-own farms as some people do, you might well take home a portable freezer full of enough soft fruit to last the winter.

## Top tips for cool boxes

Cool boxes and fridges work best when they're full, so before you leave home pop a few supermarket soft drink bottles filled with tap-water in the fridge to freeze. Use these to fill up the spare space in the cool box or fridge. Not only will you have fresh iced water to drink but you'll find all your food is cooler too, and the fridge will have used much less power to keep cool.

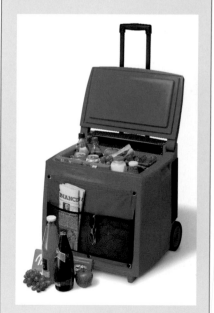

# Erecting a table

A sturdy table is essential, not just for preparing meals but also for eating them! A favourite is the roll up slatted aluminium type. These are small and light to carry but when assembled provide exactly what's required: a rock-steady and stable working surface that belies its light construction. Different models vary slightly but the principle is the same.

**1** The tables comes in a bag that will fit into any car boot and the shoulder strap makes it easy to carry on site.

**2** Folding frame and legs make up one unit. The slatted top makes another.

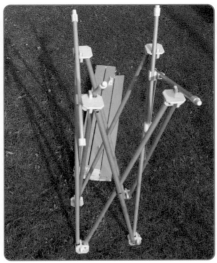

**3** Open up the frame…

**4** …until the top bars lock the legs into position.

**5** Hook one end of the tabletop onto the crossbars at the top of the frame. The slats are held together with elastic cords. Stretch them slightly to hook the other end of the table into position.

# Camping kitchens and toast!

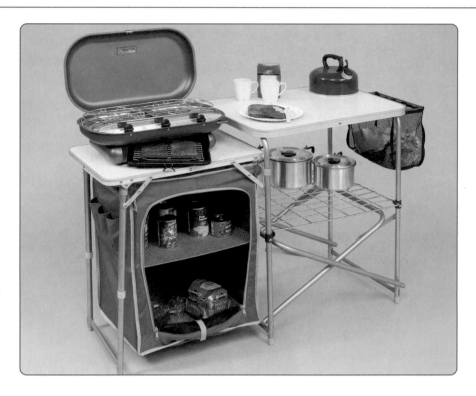

Although it's perfectly possible to cook on a small stove sat beside you on the floor, campers with larger tents, or indeed with larger families, will probably want something more convenient in the way of a camping kitchen.

You can, of course, simply put your single- or double-burner stove onto a table (preferably a metal table, as heat can damage wood or melt plastic) and do your cooking there. But the safer and more convenient option is a purpose-designed camp kitchen, of which there are many available, some of them simple, some huge and complex. You'll certainly want it to be a stable base for your cooker and you'll probably want it to provide some wind protection for cooking outdoors on a breezy day.

For this reason it's a good idea to choose a cooker and kitchen from the same manufacturer. Indeed, more and more often today you'll find kitchens designed specifically for a particular size and brand of two-burner stove.

You may want something more than a two-burner stove, and these too are available. And if you're keen on toast make sure you get yourself a stove with a proper grill.

Another requirement you might consider important is some preparation space. Though your camp table can provide a work surface it's far more convenient to have a dedicated space.

Some kitchens even provide a small washing up bowl and water supply. Trailer tenters will usually find that there's a dedicated kitchen designed specifically for their individual units, although sometimes it's an optional extra and can add considerably to the cost of a trailer tent.

Before you buy a camp kitchen of any sort, try it out. Some can be notoriously difficult to assemble or to take to pieces. Think about how easy they'll be to clean and pack. Are the shelves really useful, and will they take the kind of utensils you'll be taking

camping with you? Is the unit stable when loaded? You don't want a shaky kitchen that might deposit a saucepan of boiling water over you. Another major consideration is do you have children or dogs? How will they be around the kitchen? Will the kitchen be stable enough to resist spills if your toddler gets too close?

Normally in a camp kitchen you'll be using a stove with a connection to a gas cylinder. Where will the cylinder go? In good designs the weight of the gas bottle on a low base can add considerably to the stability, but some brands seem to have given no thought to this and you'll end up with a gas hose getting in your way every time you cook.

Some modern units are provided with bags and covers to keep the whole thing clean, neat, tidy, and easy to pack. Whether they do or not, give some thought to how you'll move the kitchen and how you'll pack it in the car.

Our last tip is one that applies to much camping equipment. Ask yourself if you really need an elaborate kitchen.

Camping equipment manufacturers have grown rich on selling spectacular-looking items – particularly kitchens – which have been taken camping once and then confined to the loft once a more simple solution has proved itself in the field.

**Above:** A more sophisticated unit provides a place to cook with covered storage for food.

**Below:** This inexpensive two burner stove also has a grill.

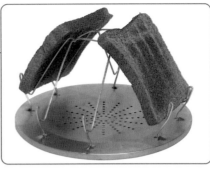

## The problems of toast

Although loads of people go camping to get away from it all and are often prepared to forgo some of the luxuries of home life, there's one facet of comfortable domesticity that every camper wants to take with them: the ability to make decent toast.

It's difficult. Camp stoves, even all singing, all dancing two-burner stoves, seldom have a good grill. But today you can find such things and the cognoscenti will assure you that a gas grill is the only way to go when it comes to toasting a white slice from delicate blonde to charcoal black or your preferred shade in between.

If you haven't a grill, what do you do? First, don't ignore the humble electric toaster. If you're the kind of camper that hooks up to the mains and you've room in your car to carry it then a simple electric two-slice toaster will produce perfect toast and make you the envy of the campsite.

However, you'll hear your neighbours whisper that this method of making toast on site is cheating and definitely out of line with the traditions of British camping. Try to ignore them as you chomp a perfect breakfast slice running with butter.

If, however, their jealousy gets to you, you may want to make toast the proper campers' way. Over the years there have been a whole range of small wire gadgets designed to hold your slice of bread at precisely the right angle, just off vertical, over the single burner of a small camp stove. Those in the shape of a ridge tent take two slices while pyramid shapes hold three or four.

These devices may win the approval of fellow campers, but in my long experience they don't make decent toast and I should know, I've bought scores of them. Some are better than others, of course, but all of them produce toast that looks like it's been carved from a zebra crossing, dark black at one end, bright white at the other.

New kid on the block is a kind of double tray made of fine stainless steel mesh. The bottom mesh diffuses the flame and the bread rests on the top mesh just the right distance from the hot flame. It certainly makes great toast. Disadvantages are that it does just one slice at a time and it needs a bit of experience to use, since it works very quickly and you'll need to keep your eye on it.

Best of all, of course, is a toasting fork – preferably carved from a green stick plucked from a nearby tree – on which you impale your slice, crumpet,

**Left:** This simple two burner stove has a grill for toast.

**Above:** This toaster stands on top of a cooking stove but making good toast with it takes practice.

**Below:** Toast on the top of the stove can be surprisingly successful using this stainless one slice toaster with its own inbuilt diffuser.

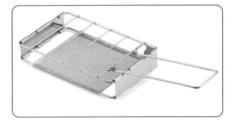

or even an old-fashioned muffin (now thankfully reappearing in the better supermarkets) to toast over your open campfire.

Wake up. Dreams like this have no place in a book on modern camp life. Sad, isn't it?

# Barbecues and instant meals

## Burning the perfect sausage

Barbecues could be the subject of a book of their own. Indeed, there are already hundreds of them. But campers who don't take a barbecue with them are missing out on one of the great aspects of outdoor living.

The dilemma with barbecues is that the best ones are generally heavy, take up a lot of room, and after their first use will invariably be dirty.

Barbecues break down into two main types: the conventional charcoal variety; and the gas-fired type, in which conventional gas flames heat either a metal grill or blocks of lava stone that replace the charcoal. Campers will argue long into the night as to which

gives the superior barbecue flavour to food. Scientific experts will tell you that in fact it's the burning fat from meat or the juice from vegetables that gives the smell and the taste, rather than any intrinsic element within the fuel itself. But who believes scientists? Those who love real charcoal will sing its praises whatever scientific opinion says.

One big advantage of charcoal is that you can add herbs, woodchips, and other flavourings to make the smoke smell wonderful, and wonderful smoke certainly *seems* to make the food taste better and probably really does. One of the biggest drawbacks with charcoal, though, is that everything about it is dirty. The charcoal itself is, and so is the ash it leaves

behind, but real fans will put up with this in exchange for what they claim is a superior flavour. Today, sealed self-lighting bags are the cleanest and best way to start a real charcoal barbecue.

Gas barbecues come in all sorts of sizes and those that use lava stones can also add herbs and woodchips to improve the aroma of the smoke and thus the food.

Instant barbecues are also available, consisting of an aluminium tray already packed with charcoal and a lighting medium. They have their own wire grid on top to take the food. Many campers will keep one ready in the car just in case they're caught out by a lovely evening and are tempted to grill the sausages or fresh sardines they're planning for tea. A dire warning on behalf of all campsite owners and wardens, though: do *not* use your instant barbecue directly on the grass. The heat will kill the turf and sterilise the earth so that nothing will grow for many months after your barbecue is forgotten.

Purpose-built stands are available for instant barbecues. Use one of these or find some bricks to protect the grass from the heat of your barbecue. Alternatively, use your instant barbecue on a paved area.

Before lighting up you should always check whether barbecues are allowed on site. In times of drought at the end of a hot summer, particularly abroad, campsite grass will be dry and inflammable and fire risk will be high. A single spark from a barbecue can and has caused serious fires.

One last note about barbecues. However delicious you make your smoke, not everyone enjoys it wafting across their tent. Check the wind

**Far left:** Various cooking tops all work with this simple grill.

**Left:** All kinds of charcoal, briquettes and lighters are available for today's barbecue chef.

direction, or better still invite your neighbours to join you for the most delicious meal of their lives.

## Instant meals

### JUST ADD WATER

Though this book isn't directly aimed at real lightweight campers concerned about every ounce they carry, it should be mentioned that a range of instant meals has been developed for them. These normally consist of dehydrated ingredients in a foil sachet. You simply cut off a corner, pour in a measured amount of boiling water, massage the bag to mix the ingredients (being careful not to spill any and scald yourself), wait for the required time, empty it into a bowl, and eat.

Stews, currys, and many similar dishes are available in this form, and so are some interesting desserts – rhubarb and custard, for instance.

These instant meals may not sound or look very appetising but some can be surprisingly delicious. Try a couple. Find some you like and keep them in your emergency stock. The night you arrive at camp four hours late and have to put up your tent in a howling rainy gale, they might be just the lifesaver that you and your family need.

**Below:** Real gourmet meals are available in sachets. The *Look what we found* range uses ingredients from small specialist farmers and fishermen to cook up delights such as Hardwick Mutton Stew and Wild Rabbit in Mustard Sauce. They just need heating.

## Why can't the flames flicker?

It's a great shame, but we seem to have lost the tradition of campfires in Britain. Most campsites just won't tolerate them. It's not as if we've got a shortage of chilly evenings when a campfire would be perfect.

The rest of the world doesn't seem to have the same problem. I've camped in the USA and Canada where every pitch on every campground has it's own fire pit. The site provides logs, often free, and in the evening friendly campers gather round each other's fires to make new friends and share camping yarns. Later in the evening when the flames have turned to glowing embers, a simple metal rack turns the fire pit into the best barbecue you've ever tasted, and your average American camper grills his steak or freshly caught trout to perfection.

In South Africa it's exactly the same, as it is in Australia and New Zealand. Our picture comes from Denmark, where, as in the rest of Scandinavia, camping isn't camping without a fire.

Because they're so popular abroad, portable fireplaces, fire braziers, and all sorts of other clever ways to have a controllable fire on a campsite, sometimes appear for sale in British camping shops.

Some campers have discovered chimniers, those pottery or cast iron furnaces that are half-way between a fireplace and a barbecue. Perhaps that's the secret: tell the warden it's a barbecue and have a sausage on a stick handy just in case he comes by to check. You might get away with it. Plenty of campers have, and perhaps if enough chimniers appear on campsites then real campfires are just around the corner.

**Above:** The romance of camping. Fire and water.

I could go on, because campfires are something I feel passionate about and I just can't understand why we don't have them here in Britain any more.

So next time you're at a campsite, ask the warden if you can have a fire and don't take 'health and safety' as an answer. If we campers demand them then perhaps site owners may realise just how good they'd be for business.

I'll certainly enjoy my next campfire. But it's a pity it'll be in the Rockies, Lapland, or Auckland, and not in England's green and pleasant land.

# Water and waste

We all take clean healthy drinking water for granted at home. Indeed, we rarely give it a thought. True, many of us now drink bottled water, but we're still used to having fresh water on tap wherever we go.

It's not quite so simple when you're camping, and you should certainly give some thought to protecting your health and welfare by ensuring that any water you use for drinking or washing is clean and wholesome. Even the smallest campsite will have a drinking tap and you can normally trust the water you get from it. That applies just as much abroad as it does here in Britain.

Traditionally, Brits abroad have

**Above:** A popular choice, this small container has a fitted tap.

**Below:** This useful water bag is easy to carry and can be hung up near your camp kitchen. It takes up hardly any space when empty.

**Below right:** Water purifying tablets are useful if you are worried about the quality of drinking water. Follow instructions very carefully.

tended to distrust the drinking water, and we're not the only ones. Did you know that French schoolchildren are warned not to drink the water when they come to Britain on holiday?

Later in this section we'll talk about moving and storing water, but whatever containers you use you need to be aware that any water in a container – particularly one that lets in light – can develop algae or bacterial growths, so it's a good idea to get into the habit of washing out all containers using a suitable chemical.

Camping shops sell tablets and fluids for this purpose and similar

chemicals are available from chemists, who usually sell them to home beer and wine makers. An excellent liquid product for this purpose is Milton, sold mainly for rinsing out baby's bottles. If it's good enough for baby it's probably good enough for you. The domestic water filter jugs that many people use at home can improve campsite water too.

Be careful with hoses used to fill containers. They really should be food quality hoses and fittings, and whatever they're made from make sure they're clean and that the ends don't get dragged through puddles or dipped into drains when you're getting ready to fill your containers.

Water is heavy and moving it from tap to tent requires some thought. Camping shops sell all kinds of bottles, jerrycans, and even folding containers. They come in all sorts of sizes and the larger ones are often fitted with convenient taps. For even larger quantities you can find products such as the Aquaroll. This is simply a tank that, when filled with water, can be fitted with a handle and rolled to your pitch.

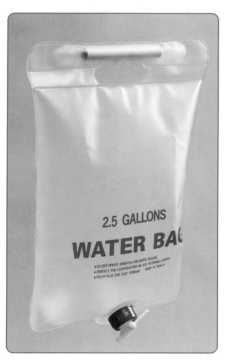

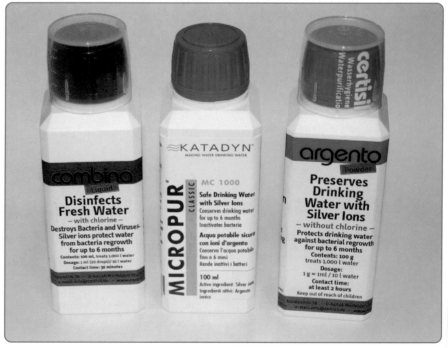

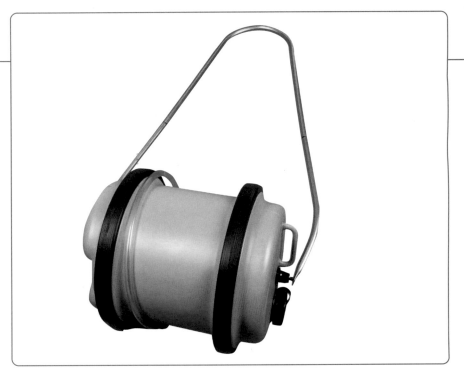

**Above:** The Aquaroll enables you to move large quantities of fresh water from the campsite tap to your tent.

**Below:** A trolley on wheels can make carrying water child's play.

Don't miss out on the simpler solutions. All the major supermarkets sell big bottles of drinking water. They're easy to pack and can fill up small spaces in the back of the car. Once you've drunk the water you can refill them and the cost is only measured in pennies.

Waste water needs some thought too, and some careful advice. Strictly speaking even the cleanest waste water should be tipped down a proper drain, but on a campsite where recently planted trees were dying from drought during a hot summer I confess that I've watered them if I've got some cleanish water to dispose of. Use your head.

When it comes to moving waste water you can find tanks with wheels that make moving large, heavy quantities of water from your tent to the campsite drain much easier. Wheeled trolleys are also available on which you can fix your jerrycan, either to obtain clean water from the tap or to carry your waste water away.

One thing to be very careful of: don't mix fresh and waste water. It goes without saying but I'll say it anyway: never use the same container for fresh and waste water however well you think you can clean them.

The best campsites will have a drinking water tap well away from it's waste water drain, and the waste drain will have it's own flushing tap. Make sure you use the right tap and drain for the right purpose. And never *never* take your chemical toilet anywhere near either of those taps, for filling, flushing, or cleaning. Always use a dedicated chemical toilet point or bring the water to the chemical toilet in a container dedicated to that use.

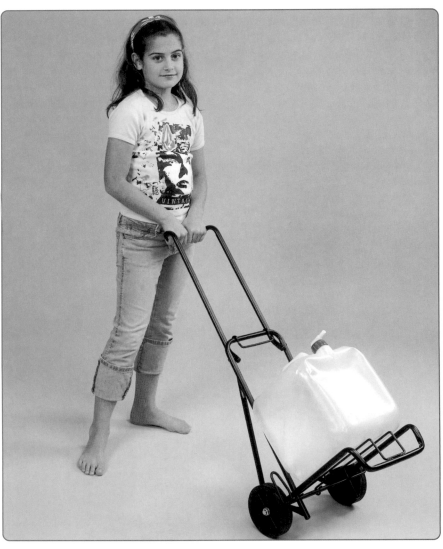

# Chemical toilets, fluids, and toilet tents

## Skip to the loo – or bring your own

We had to come to the chapter on toilets eventually, and here it is. It's strange really: so often when people discuss their camping experiences it all comes down to toilets and toilet talk. The difference between a really great campsite and one you'll never want to visit again is just how good are the toilets?

If you're using toilets on a campsite then really all you've got to do is make sure you choose a site with good facilities; but if you're camping wild or on small undeveloped sites then you'll need to take your toilet with you and there are many ways this can be done. The abbreviation 'Own san. req'd' in a

site guide or camping magazine means you'll need to bring your own toilet.

Elsan is a name well known to older campers. They invented camping toilets. In the early days these were little more then a galvanised bucket fitted with a handsomely varnished wooden toilet seat and lid, earning themselves the sobriquet 'bucket'n'chuck it'. But today things are more sophisticated. Both Elsan and their biggest rival, Thetford, make stylish portable toilets with a normal pan quite like the one you have at home. A tank holds water for flushing and the waste goes into a detachable holding tank that keeps all the unpleasantness out of sight and can be taken to a chemical disposal point for easy emptying.

Such toilets come in various sizes based on their capacity, and choosing one is always a balance between fitting it in the boot of the car – for which you need the smallest model – and being comfortable in use, for which you'll want something larger. The choice is yours.

All portable toilets use a special fluid that comes in two different kinds, although there are a score of different makes. Originally, chemical toilet fluids were based on formaldehyde and were coloured blue. Formaldehyde is a powerful chemical, and although it's not very good for you or the environment it does work, and works well, and is still a popular choice. But the more modern and more environmentally friendly fluids use enzymes to digest the waste. They're better for the planet but not so efficient at keeping waste tanks pure and sweet-smelling while you're at camp.

Traditional formaldehyde products being blue, the more environmentally friendly ones are, as you'd expect, green. But it's not quite that easy. Some environmentally 'green' products are coloured blue to give the impression

**Above:** There is a large range of sizes and styles of chemical toilets to choose from.

**Below:** How it works. Water in the holding tank flushes into the holding tank beneath.

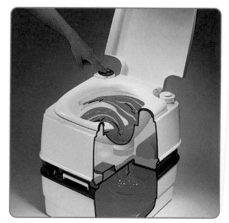

**Left:** A range of toilet tents is available. They are easy to put up and will give you the privacy you require. The double tent in the picture can recreate the side by side country privies of old. Sadly, they are more likely to be used for a single chemical toilet and a table with a basin for washing.

**Below:** The Lotus flower. We have lined the toilet bowl with three strips of toilet tissue and used three different colours to show exactly how it is done.

Once you've learned this technique you'll thank *The Camping Manual* and its author every time you make serious use of your loo.

that they're more powerful than they really are. Other tank fluids come in other colours, even purple, but don't get them confused with a totally different kind of fluid, generally pink, that you put into the flush water tank to deodorise and give a sweet smell to every flush.

The label will tell you what kind of chemical toilet fluid you're buying. Generally formaldehyde-based products will keep working for many days in the tank, whereas an enzyme-based fluid will stop working and need changing after perhaps three days.

Whichever kind of fluid you're using a good principle is to empty the holding tank as often as possible. Indeed, if you're only using your chemical toilet for a quick pee in the night then use no fluid at all. Just empty it every morning as the author does: that way you can use the site toilet for the main business of the day and still avoid a cold walk when nature calls in the middle of the night.

Once you've got your toilet you'll probably need a toilet tent so that you can sit in peace away from the prying eyes of other campers. Some campers with large family tents with lots of rooms and divisions will allocate one of these as an indoor lavatory, but when it come to discretion and hygiene it's not

such a good choice as a purpose-built toilet tent.

## The lotus position

Only those with strong nerves should read on. It's strange, but even long-established campers often don't really know the secrets of how to use a chemical toilet properly. No one gives them full instructions, and the subject is one of such delicacy that it's never openly discussed. But *The Camping Manual* and its author are made of sterner stuff, so here goes.

When you're using the chemical toilet for what we scientific campers know technically as Number Twos, do bear in mind that you haven't got the large volume of flushing water that you'd have with a normal plumbed-in toilet.

What you need to do is line the bowl. Take three pieces of toilet paper, each of two sheets joined together. Lay them in the bowl to form a flower shape. Our picture shows how it's done.

When you've done what you have to do, flush in the normal way and the toilet paper will disappear down the hole with the six leaves like the petals of a lotus flower closing round the deposit within. The bowl is left clean and fresh.

# Clothing

## WOMEN'S AUTUMN/WINTER OUTDOOR ADVENTURE WEAR

Before you even think about tents or other equipment, the main key to being warm and comfortable is wearing outdoor clothing suited to the weather in which you're camping.

There are literally hundreds of different garments and scores of brands. We turned to Britain's biggest serious outdoor clothing manufacturer – Regatta – to pick some items from their affordable ranges ideal for autumn or winter camping.

**Below:** The basic principle to stay comfortable is to use layers.

It's perfectly possible, of course, to mix and match from different manufacturers – most of us do – but not all fleeces will zip into all jackets, so when you're buying your first kit sticking to the same brand can be a good idea.

The basic principle for all outdoor clothing these days is layering. Lots of layers means you can strip them off when the going gets warm or add another layer or two when you're feeling chilly.

Let's start with underwear. Base leggings and roll-neck top worn next to the skin are both from Regatta's own Hydro-term polyester fabric, which has

excellent wicking performance – that means that if you do get hot and sweaty, the fabric will soak up the perspiration and you'll stay comfortable.

Next comes a fleece jacket made from Polartec Classic 200 fleece. It has an interactive zip so that it can be zipped into a Regatta interactive jacket for a snug fit. If may fit other jackets too, but you can never be sure. Certainly for jackets and fleeces you should always stick to one brand. You'll often find that you can buy the two together as one item and save a little money.

Outdoor trousers come in Regatta's Outdoor System polyester/cotton fabric,

BASE

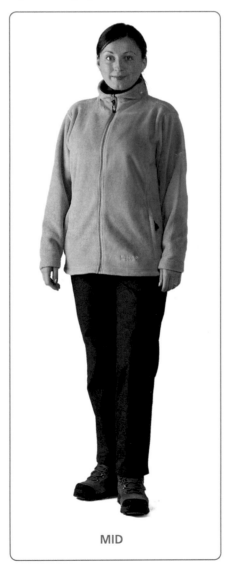

MID

OUTER

## Recycled fleece

Would you believe that many top-of-the-range and expensive camping fleeces are made from recycled plastic bottles? It's hard to believe that these soft and silky garments started life holding something like diet ginger beer, but it's true. If you're keen to do your bit for the planet always make a point of buying such recycled fleeces.

which is a soft fabric with a durable water repellent finish. These trousers feature a number of very practical pockets – campers can never have enough of these!

The waterproof and breathable jacket is made from Regatta's Isotex 8000 coated double ripstop polyester, with their own durable water-repellent finish. This fabric offers exceptional breathability and will keep rain and even light s now out.

The waterproof and breathable overtrousers are made from Regatta's Isotex coated polyester fabric with water repellent polymide liner. Not only do these overtrousers feature a leg gusset for freedom of movement but also a zip gusset right up to the knee, with adjustable Velcro tab at the ankle. This really helps in pulling them on over bulky boots.

Socks are very important. Warm, dry socks can be the difference between enjoying a weekend camping and having a miserable time. Today, outdoor socks are very hi-tech indeed. Regatta tell us that their CoolMax trekking sock is made up of 68 per cent CoolMax (polyester), 19 per cent cotton, 11 per cent nylon, and 2 per cent lycra with CoolMax for moisture control.

Wow – all that for a sock! The key thing is to find some outdoor socks you like and buy as many pairs as you can afford and can carry.

Hat, gloves, and scarf all come in a fleece fabric too. For these items it's important to pick a fleece that won't pill (ie won't develop those annoying little bobbles that can appear on fleece garments). Hats and gloves, etc, aren't fashion accessories when you're camping: they're essential in keeping your extremities warm.

Boots and shoes are dealt with on page 110, but the boot worn here is Regatta's top-of-the-range X-ert Performance suede/mesh walking boot with a full Isotex 5000 bootee for excellent waterproof protection. They're designed to provide good traction and are suitable for many different kinds of country walking. They need no breaking in.

Although we've used women's clothing as our example of autumn and winter camping wear, everything we've said also applies to men's and children's clothing. Lots of layers is the key, so that you can adjust your comfort level to the changeable weather.

# Clothing

## MEN'S SPRING/SUMMER OUTDOOR ADVENTURE WEAR

On the previous two pages we looked at the clothes and outdoor kit you need to keep warm and comfortable in the autumn and winter. Hopefully, in spring and summer the problem is a slightly different one: keeping cool and comfortable.

This is where layering really comes into its own. In the heat of the afternoon, like every other camper,

**Below:** Even in summer layers can make clothing more comfortable whatever the weather

you'll be in shorts and T-shirt or, if it's really hot, in your swimming cozzie. But as the sun goes down and the temperature drops you can pile on extra layers to keep out the chill.

We're looking at the affordable Regatta range again, though this time we've chosen to equip a man. His T-shirt is made from Comfort Control polyester/cotton with Sunshade, which offers high UV protection to reduce sunburn and worse through your clothing. Comfort Control fabrics are advanced synthetic blends that offer superb comfort and performance,

transferring moisture vapour away from the skin.

The Heaney Check Shirt worn over the T-shirt is made from peached polyester/cotton.

Today, many campers wear zip-off trousers. These can be turned into shorts simply by unzipping the legs, and if your knees get a little chilly you can zip them back on again in an instant. These zip-off trousers come in Regatta's Outdoor System polyester/cotton fabric, which has a soft finish. The key thing about this fabric is that it too offers UV protection, as well as a durable water-repellent finish. These trousers also feature a number of practical pockets.

BASE

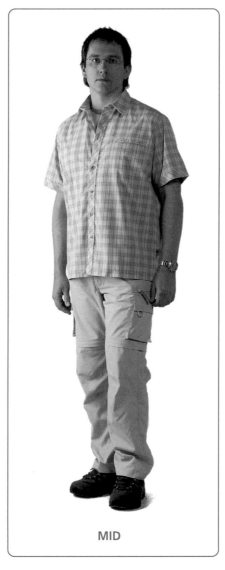

MID

OUTER

The fleece bodywarmer is made from Polartec Classic 200 anti-pill fleece. This is an ideal garment, providing warmth for the body whilst keeping the arms free.

Socks are just as important in the summer, and hi-tech varieties like these CoolMax trekking socks will keep your feet cool and comfortable.

The cap is excellent protection against the sun. This one has a Teflon coating that's stain and water resistant.

The outdoor shoes worn here have lightweight breathable suede and mesh uppers with a wicking lining. They're suitable for walking, light hiking, or just travel.

Of course, you can remove all the problems of worrying about what to wear and save a great deal of money by joining the Naturists.

Nudist camps might be the standard fare of seaside picture postcards or *Carry On* films, but they're also surprisingly popular, both here in Britain and even more so in France and other European countries.

Did you know that one in five holiday-makers in the newly fashionable Croatia go there to get their kit off? And the vast majority of them spend their holidays under canvas.

**OUTER**

Spend any time on a campsite and at least some of it will involve walking on wet grass. Choice of footwear is important if you're to remain comfortable.

Comfort doesn't always mean dry feet, however. That champion of all things camping, David Bellamy, will tell you that the best thing about camping is feeling the wet grass between the toes of your bare feet!

Many campers, of course, swear by going barefoot and who are we to discourage them, but we should issue a warning and perhaps a plea. Campsites can be littered with hidden tent pegs or worse, so if you're keen to go barefoot do take care and keep an eye out for hidden dangers.

And the plea? Make sure you leave your pitch clean and tidy when you go. Check carefully that all your pegs have

**Right:** Fabric based boots are lighter than leather.

**Far right:** Today's walking sandals are comfortable

been pulled up. If you break a glass or cup on site, be very careful that you pick up all the pieces. In the case of campsite pitches, don't just think about the appearance of the site; think about the next user and their barefoot children.

If bare feet aren't for you – and they certainly aren't for everybody – then a good pair of waterproof shoes or boots which keep your feet warm and dry. Today there's a whole assortment of footwear mostly designed for walking that works just as well on campsites.

Walking sandals have become increasingly popular over the last few years. These are a kind of half-way stage between going barefoot and wearing good protective foot wear, and they work very well indeed. However, some people find that their feet need to get used to the straps, and for some folk exposing their feet to the air can lead to the skin cracking, particularly around the heel. If so, you'll find lots of good foot creams available at a local chemist that will often sort the problem out in a matter of days.

**Above:** Our author with sandals and socks!

Now for the most contentious idea in the whole *Camping Manual*. It's possible – it isn't even illegal – to wear socks with sandals as your author shows here. Everyone else in the campsite will probably point and laugh and will certainly talk about you when you're out of sight, but it's a cure for cracked heels if only you can endure the social stigma.

Walking shoes and walking boots come in all kinds of weights and there are styles for both men and women as well as the more common unisex variety. Many lightweight boots are built like trainers and the use of silicone sprays can make them just as waterproof as the traditional proofed leather variety.

Even leather boots are lighter and more comfortable to wear than they used to be. Many need no breaking in and the choice between leather and synthetic fabrics is one of style, comfort and, of course, price.

Gore-tex and similar linings will make any kind of boot absolutely waterproof without making your feet sweaty, and that's important.

Don't ignore traditional wellie boots, now available in a remarkable range of colours and styles from fashionable all-over daisy prints to the huntin', shootin', and fishin' upmarket variety in colours to match your Range Rover upholstery – and that's just for grown-ups. You can find ladybirds, frogs, and an Ark-load of other creatures to grace your children's feet. Increasingly these more funky styles are arriving in grown-up sizes too.

Wellies have the advantage that you can stand them by the tent door and slip them on for a quick dash to the shower block, but you should avoid wearing them for too much serious walking, as blisters will result unless they're very well fitted and specifically designed for the job.

Dutch campers – and everyone in the Netherlands seems to be a camper – love their clogs, and a surprising number of Brits have also discovered just how practical this slip-on but waterproof variety of footwear can be on camp. Traditional totally wooden Dutch clogs take a lot of getting used to, but the kind with leather tops and wooden soles make great camping footwear that's quite stylish enough for a trip to the most fashionable shops in town.

Clogs are very much a matter of personal taste. Some of us just can't get on with them, but if you grow to like them you'll find that you'll never want to wear any other kind of footwear again.

Whatever kind of shoes or boots you choose, you're likely to need socks. Camping shops have racks and racks of specialist socks but these are mostly designed for various kinds of hard walking. You'll probably find that the socks you wear for the rest of the week are exactly what you need for camping weekends and holiday breaks, but do take plenty with you. Wet grass between your bare toes may be delightful but damp socks are as bad as it gets.

**Below left:** Walking boots made in traditional leather.

**Below centre:** Wellies come in all sorts of styles and colours.

**Below right:** Traditional outdoor footwear meets the fashion clog.

# Hats, gloves, and sunglasses

The reason your head is covered with hair is because it's nature's way of regulating temperature. When it's cold, most heat leaves our bodies via the top of the head and wearing a warm hat can make all the difference between feeling comfortable and feeling cold and miserable.

Campers were once traditionally known as the 'woolly hat brigade', and there's still a lot to be said for a woolly hat that can be pulled down to keep your ears snug. But today's campers have a vast choice of hats available to them, ranging from the practical through the fashionable to the hilarious and downright crazy. However they look, make sure they're good at keeping you warm.

Gloves or mittens are important too, because it's extremities that really feel the cold and lose the most heat. If you can keep your head, feet, and fingers warm the rest of your body will generally look after itself.

But all this talk of keeping warm is depressing. Hats can also have a much nicer purpose and that's to keep the sun off. A large floppy hat on a bright sunny day will not only increase comfort but will be a real factor in promoting long-term health. All of us

are becoming justifiably concerned with personal health risks and a bright sunny day has real dangers when you're out in the open air. Whether it's heat exhaustion, sunburn, or even the risks of dangerous skin cancers, a sunhat or other suitable headwear will be your first important line of defence.

If it's hot you'll be tempted to walk about in swimwear, brief shorts, or skimpy tops – or perhaps even no top at all. If you do, remember to protect yourself from the sun. You'll spend a lot more time in the open air when camping and your skin will need a lot more protection than usual. So remember the message: slap on the

high factor sun cream and try to cover up as much as possible.

Your eyes will need protection too. Wear sunglasses, of course, but also shade your eyes with a wide-brimmed hat, a baseball cap, or a sun-visor.

As well as looking after yourself, keep a careful eye on children. Again, the best advice is to keep slapping on the sun cream – of a suitably high factor – and to keep bare skin covered up where possible. When the sun is high and really strong, try to encourage children to play in the shade.

**Top:** Warm hats come in all sorts of colourful styles.

**Left:** A good sun hat will keep the sun out of your eyes.

**Below:** A good sun hat will have a wide brim.

# Maps, cases, compasses, and GPS

Many campers camp regularly without any need for maps, compasses, or modern satnav (satellite navigation) equipment. They use a road atlas or the directions in a site guide to get them to their campsite. But you can add a lot to your enjoyment of the countryside if you have the ability to use a map and a compass.

We'll only provide very basic instructions here. There are lots of specialist publications that will help you develop your map-reading skills if you want to take the subject further.

There are many kinds of maps available. Let's look at two of the most popular series, both from the Ordnance Survey: the 1:50,000 Landranger series and the 1:25,000 Outdoor Leisure and Explorer series. The 1:50,000 scale means that each 2cm square on the map represents one square kilometre on the ground, while 1:25,000 means that each 4cm represents one kilometre.

The Ordnance Survey maps divide the United Kingdom into 100km squares which form the first part of the Ordnance Survey grid reference system, each square being given two letters. Each grid squares is further divided into smaller squares by lines running vertically (called eastings) and horizontally (known as northings). This enables you to identify any square by giving the vertical grid number first, then the horizontal grid number.

To pinpoint a precise grid reference, you need to further divide your square into tenths, either by eye or by using the scale you'll find on many compasses. The number of tenths is added to the number of eastings and northings. A useful way of

remembering which comes first in a grid reference is the phrase 'along the corridor and up the stairs' – in other words, read across the map horizontally first, and then vertically (see example on right).

Maps, of course, are full of other information, and once you've located your grid reference the map will indicate interesting places to visit and walks to explore.

A simple compass can add to the usefulness of maps. It will usually come mounted in a rectangular plastic base in which the compass can be rotated through 360°. Use your compass to orientate your map. Set the housing to North. Place the compass on the map with one long edge on the north-south grid line. Rotate the map until the compass needle lines up with the compass orientation arrow on the housing. This is generally accurate enough, although you may want to allow for the magnetic variation, which will be printed on your map.

Always practise your map reading and compass work in good clear conditions on familiar ground before using them to take you out into the wild.

Do remember that your compass is magnetic, so don't use it near metal objects or close to power lines.

Today, many campers use Global Positioning Satellite (GPS) equipment, some based on pocket computers or Personal Digital Assistance (PDA). Some dedicated GPS units are now fitted to cars, either as original equipment or as aftermarket extras. Others are hand-held, though many of these also have a bracketing system that enables them to be used when driving.

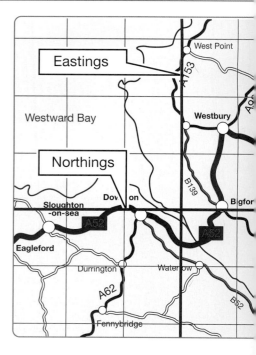

Somebody has said that GPS today is rather like mobile phones were a decade ago, and it's true that some systems are awkward to use and occasionally give most unhelpful advice and directions. But like all technologies, GPS is moving forward and each new generation is easier to use, more rugged, and more reliable, and prices are generally coming down.

**Below left:** A waterproof case, like this one from Blacks will keep maps dry and usable on the wettest day.

**Below centre:** A modern compass can be hung round your neck on a landyard.

**Below:** Know where you are and where you're going with a handheld GPS unit.

# Cameras and binoculars

This is a camping manual, not a manual on photography, but you really will be missing a whole series of tricks if you don't take a camera with you when you go camping.

Campsites and the countryside round about offer great landscapes. Kids seem to come to life on site, and the huge variety of wildlife on the average campsite will be closer and tamer than anywhere else you'll have ever been in your life.

Today, digital cameras are winning the battle against film. You'll choose whichever you prefer, but if you're still using film make sure you always have a spare reel or two with you. With digital cameras, make sure you have adequate batteries, or a charging system that will work on site. Spare batteries are a simple solution, but chargers that work from the dashboard socket of your car are also available. Plan ahead so that you don't miss that never-to-be-repeated action shot or view just because the camera batteries are flat!

Make sure you have a good weatherproof case for any camera equipment and get into the habit of keeping it in a handy place so that you'll know where to find it quickly when a great photo opportunity occurs.

Everything we've said about still cameras applies just as much to video. Indeed, today many of you will be using just one camera for both.

We've already mentioned the views and the wildlife on campsites. To get even more out of both it's worth taking a small and light pair of binoculars with you. You'll need to take into account

**Top:** Today digital cameras are winning the battle against film.

**Right:** A pair of small lightweight binoculars are always useful.

weight and size and whether the binoculars fold.

Binoculars are rated with sets of numbers, so 7x22 means that the instrument magnifies the view seven times and the front lens has a diameter of 22mm. The size of the lens is the key to how much light the binocular receives and thus how bright the image is. Sometimes you'll find more: the number 10–30x25 indicates zoom binoculars with a magnification between 10 and 30 and a 25mm front lens.

## Starring tonight

One huge bonus of camping is the chance to get away from the light pollution that plagues today's cities. A clear cloudless night on an otherwise unlit camping field will introduce you to the glories of the night sky with literally thousands of stars, not to mention planets and the moon. Some campers try to make room for a small astronomical telescope and tripod. It can provide entire evenings of entertainment.

Large magnifications can lead to problems in holding the binoculars still. Trying to follow a flying bird at very large magnification is difficult. Choose a magnification that suits the way you want to use the binoculars, and don't just go for the highest magnification available.

# Taking baby camping

How old should baby be before you take it camping? Will it be safe and happy in a tent at a few weeks, a few months, or a couple of years?

Frankly, whether a baby enjoys camping and how soon it starts is more to do with mum and dad than the baby itself. Many experienced campers have started taking their children into the great outdoors at just a few weeks, or even earlier.

If you're confident that you can keep yourself warm, dry, and comfortable then you'll be able to do the same for your offspring. However, it's a serious decision, because whereas failure could just mean a cold, wet, miserable night for you, the consequences could be far more serious if you've got baby with you.

Are you happy to deal with warming bottles, emptying potties, changing clothes, heating feeds and, of course, dealing with the inevitable nappies? – all on a campsite that, even with the best facilities, probably won't have anything like those you've got at home. That's the trade-off, and it's a decision only you can make.

Certainly today's campers will find the equipment they need to keep baby happy and comfortable easy to obtain.

There are dedicated camping buggies and other kids' kit, but in reality any of the baby superstores will provide most of the things you need to keep even the youngest camper fit and healthy, as well as warm and comfortable.

As for baby 'travel systems' – an important-sounding name for what used to be called simply a buggy or pram – today you'll find any number that build around a carrycot, ideal for baby to travel to the car before being transferred to a purpose-built and dedicated baby car-seat. Once on site the carrycot mounts on wheels, and you'll find that many systems even include undercarriages built for cross-country use. Add a few accessories to take the vast amount of kit a modern baby seems to need when travelling, and baby's camping kit is complete.

You'll need to think hard about keeping the little one warm and snug, but sleeping bags and outdoor clothing come in the smallest sizes and are often much more attractive than those offered for we poor grown-ups.

As every parent knows, children take up a lot of space as well as a lot of time, and it sometimes seems the younger the baby the more time and

space he or she seems to take. But if you love camping get the kids doing it early. That way it gets in their genes. Our son first camped at just a few weeks old, sleeping in a carrycot at the foot of our bed in a small ridge-tent overlooking the sea in Pembrokeshire. Forty years on he's taking his own children camping, and they love it just as much as their parents and grandparents do.

Once toddlers get a bit older you can really get them into the delights of camping. Even if you still want them sleeping in the main tent with mum and dad, their own small fun tent or pup tent will give them a chance to learn the skills of putting a tent up, as well as giving them plenty to do and a place to play while you have a quiet break.

Ready-erected tent companies such as Canvas Holidays offer special tents for slightly older children, and on many campsites – especially those abroad – you'll find wooden rumble trucks for the kids to move about all the things they need, including sometimes a brother or sister. What a great invention! Anything that turns a chore into a game has got to score top marks with harassed parents.

**Left:** This cross country buggy will give little ones a chance to enjoy the countryside.

**Below:** Little 'uns always love these under-bed tents that can be added to many trailer tents and folding campers. Just don't tell them that they are universally known as dog kennel tents!

# First Aid

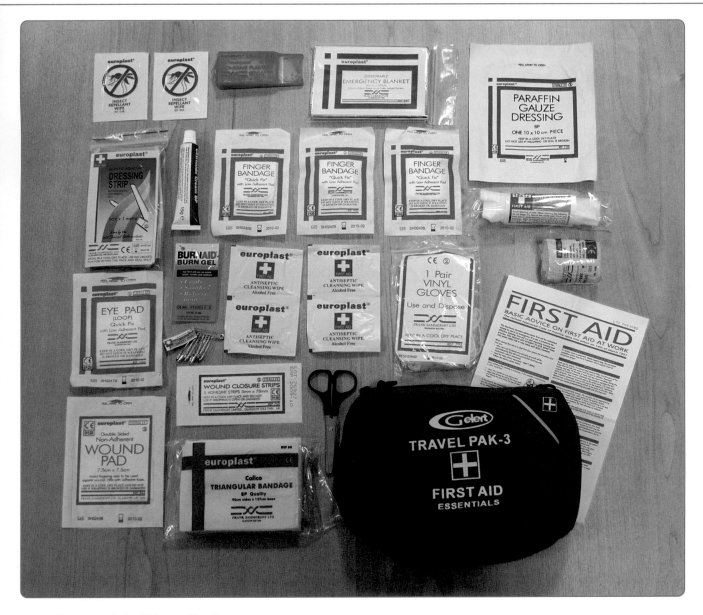

## Dealing with life's little knocks

Always have a First Aid kit to deal with simple emergencies at camp. Don't keep it sealed up until it's needed. Check what's in it and that you know how to use the contents, and read the leaflets that are usually included *before* an emergency occurs. That way you'll be prepared.

The most important thing is to remember that First Aid is precisely that. First Aid for small cuts and bruises. If you're in any doubt at all about treating the patient, or if you think there may be something seriously wrong, then seek proper medical attention immediately.

For relatively small cuts and grazes where there's minimal blood loss, you can treat the injury yourself. Clean the wound and surrounding area under running water. An antiseptic can be applied to protect against infection. Apply a plaster or dressing when the wound is dry.

On a campsite another frequent injury will be trips and falls. These soft tissue injuries should be treated following the '**RICE**' procedure:

**Above:** This first aid kit by Gelert is designed for campers.

**R** – Rest the injured part.
**I** – Apply ice or a cold compress.
**C** – Compress the injury.
**E** – Elevate the injured part.
Rest, steady, and support the injured part. Make sure the casualty is comfortable.

If the injury has just happened, cool the area by applying an icepack or a cold wet cloth – a sealed pack of frozen peas can work particularly well. This cooling can reduce swelling, bruising, and pain.

Next apply gentle, even pressure. Surround the injury with a thick layer of soft padding such as cotton wool or plastic foam, and secure it with a bandage.

Raise and support the injured limb to reduce blood flow to the injury and thus reduce bruising.

If the casualty is in a lot of pain or you suspect there may be more damage, such as a fracture or broken bone, then take them to hospital.

Yet another common campsite injury will be scalds or burns. Scalds are wet burns caused by hot liquids; burns are heat injuries caused by flames or hot surfaces. In all cases the treatment is the same. Cool the burnt area with copious quantities of cold water. Keep pouring cold water over the burnt area for as long as possible. If fresh water is in short supply you can use water from a river or pond. The important thing is to use lots and lots of it. Keep flooding the burnt area with water for as long as possible.

## The real emergencies

On these pages we've given some tips on how to cope with everyday minor incidents. However, you should always seek urgent medical help if the person:

■ Has stopped breathing.
■ Is breathing with difficulty and their lips are going blue.
■ Is unconscious.
■ Has a deep wound.
■ Is bleeding badly.
■ Has a serious burn.
■ Has a suspected broken bone.
■ Has been stung in or around the mouth.
■ Has a foreign body or a chemical in their eyes.
■ Has an eye injury caused by a sharp object.
■ Has drunk or eaten anything which you suspect may be poisonous.
■ Has been bitten by a snake.

Never, *ever* use any grease or butter on a burn. It will simply fry the skin.

Do not burst blisters. There's a risk of infection and a loss of body fluids, which is one of the most serious problems with any kind of burn. If the burn is in any way large or serious call for medical assistance.

## Animal bites

If you're bitten by any kind of animal you should always seek medical treatment. In many countries rabies is found in both wild and domesticated animals.

Rabies is a potentially fatal viral infection. Injections are available if you're bitten, but you must get medical advice quickly in order for the treatment to be effective.

First Aid for any animal bite is to wash the wound and the area around it with soap and water, pat it dry, cover it with a dry dressing, and then seek medical advice.

## Other bites

Stings from jellyfish can be painful, as can stepping on a sea urchin or some other fish. Put the injured part in water that's as hot as the casualty can bear. Vinegar in the water can help. Don't use alcohol on the sting – this will make it worse. Dry the area and use talcum powder or, if you have it, barbecue meat tenderiser, which contains papain, a protein-digesting enzyme that inactivates the venom.

## Anaphylactic shock

There is a danger of anaphylactic shock whenever someone is bitten or stung, or sometimes as a result of a food reaction. This is a serious, potentially fatal condition caused by the reaction of the body to the substances that enter it. Symptoms are anxiety, skin blotches, swelling of the face and neck, puffiness around the eyes, rapid pulse, difficulty breathing, and gasping for air.

If you suspect anaphylactic shock get emergency medical attention as soon as possible.

## The recovery position

If there are no other obvious life-threatening conditions, unconscious casualties who are breathing and who have a pulse should be put into the recovery position. This position stops the tongue from blocking the airway, and allows liquids and vomit to drain away rather than blocking the airway.

Always check the patient's mouth for obstructions such as food or dentures, and remove them.

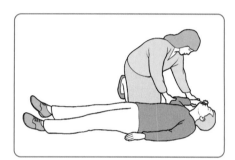

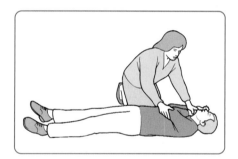

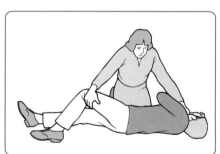

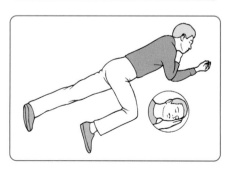

## Insect stings and bites

Bee stings are acid, so bicarbonate of soda is still a good remedy. Wasp stings are alkali so use vinegar, a mild acid, on these. If you can see the sting, remove it with tweezers.

You can reduce the pain of a sting with a cold compress or a bag of ice or a sealed bag of frozen food. Sting relief creams are available and should be in your camping kit.

You should understand the danger of a bite or sting in or near the mouth. These can lead to serious swelling that can close the air passages and make breathing difficult or even impossible. Someone stung here should be given ice to suck or sips of cold water and medical attention should be sought urgently.

One insect that may bite you is the tick. Found in grass or woodland, these attach themselves to animals and campers. They're very small and can be

**Top:** A good insect repellent is essential on some campsites at some times of year. Find one you like and that works for you – preferably before you need it.

**Right:** Even lovable lambs can carry a health risk.

virtually invisible until they start to suck your blood. Then they can swell to the size of a pea.

Ticks carry diseases – some of them dangerous. In the USA and in European countries such as Croatia, the Czech Republic, Slovenia, and Slovakia, they carry tick-borne encephalitis (TBE), a viral disease that can lead to meningitis, which in serious cases can result in paralysis and death. Remove the tick very carefully using tweezers and a gentle rocking movement. Ensure that you also remove the head and the jaws.

If you're bitten by a tick get medical advice as soon as possible. Keep the tick's body in a container so that you can take it with you when you seek medical attention. Doctors may be able to identify the particular risk, if any, from the dead tick.

## Get yourself trained

Getting yourself trained in First Aid might be a good idea. The British Red Cross Society, St John's Ambulance, and the St Andrew's Ambulance Association in Scotland all organise local courses in First Aid.

Basic courses take four to six evenings, usually one evening a week.

More comprehensive courses are also available and these will take up to four full days or the equivalent. Some employers will give their staff time off and even pay for them to go on a First Aid course.

You can find details of such courses in *Yellow Pages* or on the Internet.

## After the animals

If you camp in farmers' fields you'll sometimes find evidence of animals that have been there before you. Cattle, sheep, and other animal droppings should be avoided. They can carry infections such as E. coli, salmonella, and other nasties.

Children in particular find animal droppings fascinating, so if you do find yourself in this situation encourage your kids to wash their hands frequently. Tell them not to play with cowpats – although you might find it hard to stop them.

Make sure you wash your own hands frequently too, especially before preparing food or even pouring drinks.

An anti-bacterial hand gel, available from any chemist, is a good first line of defence against these kinds of infections.

# Multi-purpose tools and knives

Traditionally campers have always liked to have a penknife, and the more experienced the camper the more blades that penknife would have. Today, many campers still find Swiss army knives and their near relatives and imitators useful things to have.

It's possible to obtain knives with a remarkable number of blades, but in reality you'll find one with a few really useful blades, tools, and accessories far more useful and therefore much more often used than some of the extreme varieties.

A sharp penknife blade is, of course, the main reason you'll take a Swiss army knife. Add to that a small pair of foldaway scissors and a set of tweezers and you're well on your way. A Swiss army knife will also usually have a toothpick, a pen, and that absolutely essential item, a corkscrew.

But today the Leatherman multi-tool, along with its imitators and cheaper replicas, is taking over from Swiss army-style knives among many campers. These heavily-built multi-tools are based round a pair of stainless steel pliers. Various other tools, appliances and just plain gizmos fold out from the basic tool to handle a multitude of jobs. They're generally heavier-duty than multi-bladed knives, and the best of them come in a nice holster that fits on your belt so that they're always available when you need them and less likely to get borrowed or stolen.

You need to be careful when buying either knives or multi-tools. There are lots of cheap copies available, and with most of them the tools and cutting edges are, frankly, rarely up to the job. It certainly pays to buy a reputable brand if you can afford it, although the best ones can be very expensive indeed.

**Top:** The traditional Swiss army knife is still a popular choice for many campers.

**Right:** A genuine leatherman is the Roll Royce of multi-tools.

**Below:** This multi-purpose tool comes in an elegant pocket case.

## Top tip

Here's a question – do you really *need* all of your tools to fold out of a single knife or appliance? Give some thought to whether a simple tool kit of knife, pliers, scissors, and pen might not be much more flexible, more use, and indeed cheaper to buy than either a Swiss army knife or a multi-purpose tool such as a Leatherman.

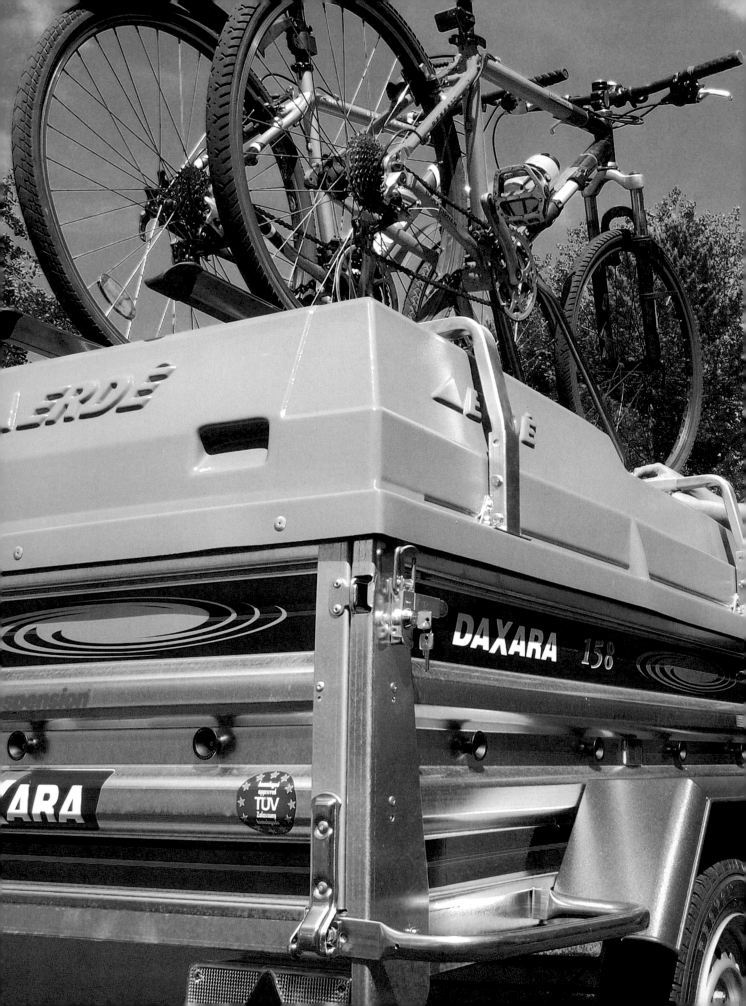

# Going camping

# 4

## Getting there with your kit

Today many campers arrive by car, and a large estate car or MPV at that, on the other hand it is quite possible to take all your camping kit on your back.

Most campers will fall somewhere between these two extremes. You can carry your gear on your back in a rucksack or fit a roof box to your car, and those who travel by pushbike or motorcycle will find special equipment in which to pack their camping gear. And if your vehicle really hasn't got enough room then hang a trailer on the back. It works for cars certainly, but you'll find motorbikes towing trailers and there are even cyclists who transport their kit this way.

# Day sacks, rucksacks, and other packs

**Left:** Different packs for different people.

objects are poking into your back. The hip strap or belt should be tightened to ensure that your hips are taking their share of the rucksack load.

## How much should you carry?

How much you can carry depends on how fit you are, of course, but a good basis for starters is that you probably won't be very comfortable carrying any more than one quarter of your body weight.

This is particularly important for young campers, who'll often feel they're capable of carrying as much as they can lift. This attitude can cause serious problems, so stick to the table below.

A 7-stone (50kg) person can carry 25lb (12kg).
An 8-stone (58kg) person can carry 28lb (14kg).
A 9-stone (65kg) person can carry 30lb (16kg).
A 10-stone (72kg) person can carry 35lb (18kg).
A 12-stone (86kg) person can carry 43lb (21kg).
A 14-stone (100kg) person can carry 50lb (24kg).
A 16-stone (116kg) person can carry 56lb (28kg).

## What size?

Rucksacks in Britain are measured in litres. In the USA they're measured in cubic inches.

Today, rucksacks and daysacks come in a remarkably wide range of sizes and styles. Indeed, even glamorous supermodels have given up handbags in favour of super-stylish backpacks, while office workers are just as likely to carry their laptops in a backpack as in a conventional briefcase.

If you're planning to take all your camping kit with you on your back

## Carrying it on your back

It's perfectly possible to carry everything you need for a camping holiday on your back. Thousands of backpackers do it all the time and today there are sizes and styles of rucksack to suit everybody's needs.

When you're choosing a rucksack think about size of course, but also think about what kind of person you are. Would you be happy to put everything inside the bag and search through it when you need something? Or are you the kind of person who'd like a pocket for everything and everything in its place?

Packing a rucksack is certainly a science and some would describe it as an art in its own right. The basic principle is to get the heavy items as close to the spine and as high as possible. This weight distribution brings maximum comfort.

Also, think about the order in which you need to *un*pack. The flysheet should be on top of the tent and both

should be on top of the sleeping bag. Make sure that items such as bedding and clothing are protected against rain and damp, and try to ensure that the pack is well balanced, with weight equally distributed on both sides.

Outside pockets should be used for items such as stoves and fuel, so that smells and leaks do not affect everything within the bag. Cooking and eating equipment too, as well as food, should be kept in separate bags and, ideally, packed away in outside pockets.

Your waterproof coat should always be packed in a way that ensures it's easily accessible.

Once you've worked out a way of packing that you're happy with, stick to it and try to make it a habit. That way you'll know where to look when you need an item in a hurry.

A fully loaded rucksack is quite cumbersome until it's hoisted onto the shoulders. Be careful you don't bump it and damage the frame. Make sure the straps are adjusted so that the rucksack can't roll and always check that no hard you'll probably be looking for a 65-plus litre rucksack, and campers will also require a daysack to take wet-weather gear, cameras, drinks, etc, when they venture off site for a walk or a day out.

## Pockets or not?

Some people like rucksacks with pockets, some don't. If you're a backpacker and you're going to travel by public transport side pockets can become a pain. They snag in doorways and catch on fellow travellers on trains and buses. A slim pack no wider than you are will be much easier in such situations.

Some rucksacks offer a choice of one or two compartments. When you have two you can keep wet clothes and tent separate from dry clothing.

## One for the kids

It's a good idea to encourage kids to carry their own gear. Sort out a small rucksack like these adventure packs from Gelert and not only will your children enjoy being part of the camping party but they'll also learn practical lessons as future campers. Children always want to take far too much on a camping holiday, and getting them to carry it on their backs is a good way of getting them to realise how little they really need.

## Packing your rucksack

This is a 65-litre Vango Sherpa rucksack, with some suggestions on how to pack it.

1. Small torch, tissues, lipsalve, sunscreen, sunglasses, maps, sweets, and all those other bits, preferably in a bag.
2. First Aid kit. See page 116 for contents.
3. Your waterproof jacket and trousers and your towel.
4. Your tent, or your bits of the tent if there's more than one of you using the same tent and sharing the carrying.
5. Water-bottle and lightweight food. Small bottle of washing-up liquid, well wrapped in a plastic bag: this must be packed in one of the pockets, as a leak of detergent can ruin waterproofs and tents.
6. Stove and matches in the other pocket.
7. Fuel for stove, placed in a pocket to avoid liquid fuel leaks tainting food or equipment.
8. Clothes, underwear, socks, and sandals.
9. Washbag.
10. Cooking pan or pans, cutlery, and mug, either wrapped in or stuffed with loose clothing or tea towels.
11. Sleeping mat.
12. Sleeping bag and liner.

Things like tent poles and spare footwear can be strapped to the outside of the rucksack. Travel documents, passports, etc, and cameras are probably more secure carried on your person rather than in your rucksack.

This packing plan is just a starting point. Over time you'll develop your own system for packing everything in your rucksack.

## How will you get to your campsite?

For most people the answer to this question will be by family car. Few people will have the luxury of being able to afford a car just for camping outings.

If you're a regular camper, give some thought to the room your car offers. Estate cars work best for camping, but today many small hatchbacks offer a remarkable amount of boot space, and many makers offer features such as a 12-volt socket in the boot which will make running your fridge or cool box easy when camping.

There are several ways you can increase the amount of camping gear your car will carry, including a roof rack, a roof box, or perhaps a bike rack mounted on the rear. But if you're carrying bikes on the back of your car, remember that you need to give the driver behind a clear view of your lights, indicators, and number plate. Often this will require an additional lighting board mounted on the back of your load.

Motorcyclists will need to choose lighter and more compact camping gear, but it's perfectly possible to find specially made luggage that will enable you to carry everything you need on a motorbike. Indeed, some motorcycle manufacturers such as BMW even supply camping equipment, tents, and luggage as part of their accessory range.

It's perfectly legal to tow a trailer with your motorcycle and to find more details of how this can be done legally and safely see the panel opposite.

Even lighter equipment is required if you're travelling by bike. Purpose-built luggage is available, and with a pair of rear panniers, front panniers, and both saddlebag and handlebar bag it's remarkable how much camping equipment can be carried on an ordinary bike.

Finally, of course, we have backpacking, where everything you need is carried in a rucksack on your back. However, *The Camping Manual* doesn't set out to be a guide for backpackers, since there are already many other books that deal with this subject in great depth. But be warned: many of them are written for the American market and you may find that the equipment within is unavailable in Britain.

When I started preparing for this book I went on to the Amazon website. This offered a dozen books on camping. All were of American origin and a third of them were historical reprints describing camping as it was as much as a century ago. Virtually every book described how to deal with a rattlesnake bite but not one even mentioned how to bring mains electricity into a family framed tent. Hence *The Camping Manual*.

**Above:** A roof box like this one from Thule can add useful carrying space to any size of car. Bikes can travel on an outside rack but always check your car handbook to ensure you remain within safe load limits.

**Below:** This family share out the equipment into well packed panniers on a whole range of bikes.

# Camping trailers

## Trailers can carry a lot

The most common solution to the problem of insufficient space in your car for camping equipment is the simple trailer. In fact they're sometimes even called camping trailers, which has become a generic name for trailers that are frequently used for such other purposes as carrying garden waste and building materials.

The market is dominated by small and light metal trailers, often of French design but increasingly being made in the Far East or assembled out of parts from the Far East or China. They can be fitted with a simple fabric cover or with a moulded plastic top often designed with an integral rack to take further equipment. All but the simplest come with a drop-down tailboard. This feature makes it far easier to load them, particularly with heavy items such as a camping fridge, or even some larger tents.

Moving slightly upmarket you come to the traditional wooden-sided trailer, often British made. This will have a metal frame, a plywood floor, and timber sides made from either wooden boards or plywood. Solid and well made, these trailers seem to last forever and can sometimes be found on the second-hand market.

A word of warning, however: there are some very old trailers about and some have been used only occasionally, and have never been maintained. Don't become one of those people who leave their trailer to quietly rust in the garden, only to drag it out once a year for the family holiday. Trying to tow a trailer that hasn't been serviced for years hundreds of miles to your favourite camping destination is a surefire way to get your holiday off to the worst possible start. We've all seen them, the sad family stood by the car blaming Dad for not checking the tyres or wheel bearings or, indeed, anything else before he set out.

There's a lot more information on trailers, towing, maintenance, and trailer security in the section on trailer tents and folding campers on page 59.

If you really want to become a trailer expert then a good place to start is the *Haynes Trailer Manual* by Brian Bate. This is a complete guide to buying, maintaining, and even building light trailers suitable for carrying camping equipment.

**Above:** A good camping trailer can carry all you need.

## Motorcycle trailers

A solo motorcycle with an engine capacity above 125cc can legally tow a trailer. The law restricts such trailers to a maximum weight of 150kg or two-thirds of the kerb weight of the motorbike, whichever is less. It also requires the kerb weight to be clearly marked on the nearside of the motorcycle.

The overall width of the trailer must not exceed 1 metre and the distance between the rear wheel axle of the motorcycle and the rear of the trailer must not exceed 2.5 metres.

# Some other ways to go camping

**5**

Not all campers own their own equipment or use conventional tents. In the next few pages we'll talk about hiring equipment, using pre-erected tents on Continental sites like the one pictured on this page, and using tents that sit on top of your car.

Finally, we'll look at camping afloat, and return briefly to those heady days over a hundred years ago when Three Men in a Boat slept under canvas.

# Ready-erected tents

## Here's one we put up earlier

You don't have to put up your own tent at all. If you book a holiday with a company like Canvas Holidays you'll find they have pre-erected tents in countries throughout Europe – but surprisingly not in Britain.

Although one or two of the pre-erected tent companies have experimented with tents on British campsites they just don't seem to have caught on. So it's easy to rent a pre-erected tent in Croatia but not in Cumbria!

In reality, although companies like Canvas Holidays offer their tent vacations in many countries – Italy, Spain, Austria, Switzerland, Germany, Holland, and Luxembourg, as well as Croatia – the bulk of their business is sending we Brits on camping holidays to France.

Canvas Holidays started 40 years ago. In those days it was hard to find inexpensive holiday hotel accommodation in France and the French didn't seem keen to emulate their Spanish neighbours and build huge numbers of hotels and self-catering apartments for the growing British package holiday trade. Yet there was an undoubted demand in Britain for holidays in La Belle France, and that demand was satisfied by British companies putting pre-erected, British-owned tents on French-owned campsites and renting them out as part of a package.

Forty years on the procedure hasn't changed that much. You'll still probably buy a fortnight's holiday in a luxury tent on a sophisticated campsite somewhere in France. Your holiday will include a ferry crossing for you, your family, and your car, an insurance package, detailed information on your route, complete with maps, and even more information on what to do when you reach your chosen destination.

When you arrive on site you'll find a remarkably large and luxurious frame tent with proper beds in three separate bedrooms, a dedicated kitchen with cooker and fridge, and big sitting areas inside and out. You'll also find a team of couriers on site with all the local advice and information you'll need. Like all good holiday reps, they'll organise welcome parties and excursions, and will have a programme of activities for both young children and for teenagers. They'll be there to give day-to-day advice and tips, and also to help out in a real emergency.

All this will happen on a site where a big proportion of the visitors will be British, and some people see this as a mixed blessing. The staff will almost certainly speak English, the bar may well serve British beer, and when England is playing in an international football match on the satellite television in the bar you'll be able to cheer for them without worry. Everything, in fact, will be just what you'd expect from any other package holiday designed for British holidaymakers, but all under a canvas roof.

So let's have a look at what you get – and what you don't get – under that canvas roof. You get a big tent with, as we've said, three separate bedrooms, or in some cases two. The walls are moveable – they're only canvas, after all. All the beds have metal frames and proper sprung mattresses. You'll probably settle for a double in one room for yourselves, while the kids can have the three single beds in one big room or put up the divider to make two rooms, one with two beds the other with one. A further option for older children is their own small tent outside.

Your tent will have mains electricity for lights and fridge and there'll be a few mains sockets for hairdryers or the television if you've brought it. It's unlikely, however, that the television set you use at home will pick up French TV.

The tent won't have running water. Like all good campers you'll fetch that from the nearby tap or make it one of

the kids' chores. For toilets and showers you'll use the facilities block like all the other campers on site.

You'll have brought your own towels and bed linen. This is no problem if

you've come by car, but as cheap flights become more popular firms like Canvas Holidays are offering linen hire to those who choose to travel by air.

Let's look outside the tent. Here you'll find a large sun-awning offering somewhere shady to sit on the sun-loungers provided. Indeed, if it's a very open site with little natural shade you can organise a gazebo to provide somewhere roomy out of the sun.

Finally, the company provides every tent with that essential accessory of all British campers abroad – a charcoal barbecue.

# Roof rack tents

## Upstairs to bed

Rooftop tents have always been popular with Land Rover and other 4x4 owners. They were developed in Africa, where their main purpose was to stop a sleeping camper becoming supper for lions, jackals, or similar beasts. From there they gradually spread to less dangerous camping country, and although they're still mostly popular with owners of big four-wheel-drive vehicles some of the new and lighter models are suitable for family saloons and estates.

A good example is the Oasis 2 featured on these pages. It's a French design with a metal frame and a Chinese-made proofed nylon tent. 4x4

Touring Gear of Bedford imports it into Britain as part of a range of rooftop tents that they can supply.

Rooftop tents are still quite novel and you'll certainly cause a stir when you arrive at your campsite, but because they need no pegging and have their own bed inside you can sleep in them in the most unlikely locations and you don't need a grassy site to be comfortable.

The Oasis 2 mounts on a car roof rack but has its own metal frame, which when unfolded is effectively a sprung double camp bed 2.4m long by 1.4m wide, and the tent itself is 1.2m high. The slightly upturned end of the bed saves on pillows and gives a comfortable sleeping position. The

**Above:** Roof tents come in an amazing variety of sizes.

Oasis has a large door each side and lots of ventilation. In all but the hardest weather it works perfectly as a single-skinned tent, but there's an elasticated flysheet in silver reflective nylon that gives added protection if the weather is harsh, or welcome reflective insulation if the weather gets too hot.

We fitted the Oasis to an excellent family camping car, the Volvo V50 estate. This may be stylish and even racy looking, but it has no less than three 12-volt sockets inside, which proves that those Swedish designers have thought about us campers.

# Fitting the roof rack

**2** It's important that the roof rack bars are parallel and exactly 90cm apart.

**1** Our Volvo came with these stylish and aerodynamic roof bars. They cause no wind noise, but sadly they were too wide for the brackets that held our roof tent in position.

**3** These roof rack bars are also genuine Volvo parts but much more utilitarian, and they fitted our rooftop tent clamps perfectly.

**4** These U-bolts hold the tent frame to the roof rack.

**5** They can be cut to length to neaten the job.

# The Oasis 2 tent

These small clips tension the tent covering.

The elasticated flysheet offers additional protection from rain or bright sunshine.

## Warning

Before you think about putting a roof tent on your car, it's essential you check the maximum loading in the car manufacturer's handbook. Don't forget it's not just the weight of the tent but the weight of the sleeping campers and all their equipment needs to be taken into account too.

Large doors and good mesh covers offer excellent ventilation.

Inside the tent is snug and comfortable.

The base, like a good camp bed, is sprung with rubber lacing.

The whole unit weighs just 14kg.

# Putting the tent into position

**1** The Oasis 2 in its travelling cover ready for mounting on our Volvo.

**2** Two adults can easily lift it into position.

**3** Once clamped in place you can drive with it anywhere.

**4** When you arrive on site, off comes the travelling cover…

**5** …and one end is unfolded.

**6** Then the other.

**7** The tent is up. The aluminium ladder travels under the folded tent on the roofrack.

**8** The Oasis 2 is ready for a good night's sleep.

**9** You can still get full access to the boot.

# Tents that hang on the back of cars

If you have a large car, perhaps a four-wheel drive, you may want to use the inside of it as part of your camping accommodation. There may be room in the car for you or your children to sleep, or you may do your cooking or washing in the boot under a canvas cover that's part of a tent that hangs on to the vehicle itself.

If that sounds like your kind of camping you're in luck, for there's a whole range of tents that fit on to your car and link accommodation under canvas with extra accommodation inside your vehicle. Land Rover even produce a range of such tents as luxury accessories for their various vehicles. The Land Rover solution is, in fact, a

**Above:** Land Rover supply a branded tent to use with their vehicles.

**Below:** The Caranex, made in Scotland, comes in a variety of sizes to fit cars large and small.

free-standing tent linked by a large sleeve into which the back of the car can be fitted.

Specialist tent manufacturers can also provide various add-on tents to suit cars and vans of any size from the smallest hatchback up.

The advantages of such a tent are obvious. The car provides a sturdy framework that can help support the tent, and on windy days when others are watching their canvas homes with concern you'll be delighted that your bedroom is anchored to a motor car that's unlikely to be blown over in even the strongest wind.

When car and tent are being used together you can easily plug equipment into the car's 12-volt system and use it either in the tent or in the back of the car. Your camping fridge, for instance, can travel in the boot wired to a 12-volt socket and stay there when you're on site, avoiding any heavy lifting. You'll still be able to reach food and drink stored in the fridge easily, and the same thing may well apply to other kitchen facilities that can be likewise used in the boot.

There are two sides to every story, however, and these tents have a downside too. If you're planning to leave the site temporarily, some tents will need to be taken down or at least laid flat, and every time you return from the shops, the pub, or the restaurant do you really want to have to put the tent up again, however easy it is?

To get round that problem many of

these units can be supplied with extra poles so that you can disconnect and drive away while leaving the tent standing on site. These poles are often sold as extras, and if you're going down this route it might be worth considering whether a conventional, and probably a less expensive, type of tent might be a more suitable option.

However, a long-established maker of this kind of tent – Caranex – has sold thousands of units and their enthusiastic owners wouldn't consider anything else.

This kind of tent is best suited to travellers who spend most of their time moving from campsite to campsite and stop in a different location each night. They're usually quick to pitch, and in the morning you can take down the tent, stuff it into the boot of your car, and be gone. The next night you'll be in a different location many miles away.

Such tents are closely related to caravan and motorhome awnings and owners of large people carriers and MPVs may find that an awning designed for a small motorhome could suit them and their vehicle perfectly.

Perhaps the Rolls Royce of this kind of camping unit is one that combines a rooftop tent with a back annex that can even, in the largest models, offer room for a toilet and shower. Truthfully, however, you're more likely to see that kind of camping in the African bush or the Outback down under than on a campsite in the Home Counties.

# Camping on the water

## Three men in a boat

Everyone knows Jerome K. Jerome's story of the three men who took their camping skiff up the Thames and didn't forget the dog. Amazingly, although the story is well over a century old you can still hire beautiful wooden camping skiffs on the Thames, as well as on some other rivers.

This nineteenth-century way of travelling and camping is certainly making a comeback. Can there be a better way of shaking off the stress of our modern age? Even without experience you'll find the boats just as easy to handle as Jerome K. Jerome did in 1889.

So just what is a camping skiff? Well, it's a wooden rowing boat about 6m (24ft) long. It's easy to row and holds three people and a dog. At night a canvas cover converts the whole craft into a snug tent with room for three friendly people to sleep on board using simple mats and sleeping bags just as in any other tent. A small stove will enable you to cook breakfast on the bank and washing is usually dealt with by a dip in the river first thing in the morning.

Traditionally meals will be taken at riverside hostelries, and, like Jerome and those who've followed in his wake ever since, you may want a break from the fairly rudimentary accommodation that a camping skiff offers. Whisper it quietly, but there are riverside bed-and-breakfasts available, or you can pack a more comfortable tent to stop at a riverside campsite and enjoy some more luxurious ablutions than a simple bankside mooring might offer.

You can expect to travel 10 to 20 miles a day depending on your level of fitness and just how much of a hurry you're in. Riverside pubs can be tempting, and long lunches can certainly cut down the mileage. Even so, you can cover the most picturesque parts of the Thames on a pleasant week-long holiday.

Many of the original Thames skiffs are still for hire. Some are more than a hundred years old but still offer a great holiday experience. Try Mark Edwards at the Richmond Bridge Boat Houses. Contact Tom Balm on 020 8948 8270 for more details of this really original way to go camping.

## More camping afloat

More modern boats can be used for camping too. A large and stable sailing dinghy, such as the long-established Wayfarer Class, will have plenty of room for all your camping equipment, and you can even sleep in the dinghy under a specially-made tent that uses the sailing rig boom as its ridge pole.

Many members of the UK Wayfarer Association use their boats in this way. You can contact them and find out much more on their website at www.wayfarer.org.uk.

The Dinghy Cruising Association also has lots of members who use all kinds of sailing dinghies for camping, and has an excellent website with lots of information on how to go camping afloat safely and comfortably. Visit them at www.dca.uk.com.

## Broads camping craft

Thames Skiffs aren't the only traditional camping watercraft available for hire. On the Norfolk Broads, for instance,

**Above left:** For over a hundred years skiff campers have been exploring the Thames.

**Above:** Cooking in the skiff is by a simple two burner stove.

**Below:** These halfdeckers on the Norfolk Broads offer fine sailing and comfortable tented overnight accommodation.

you've always been able to hire traditional sailing boats known as half-deckers, about 16ft (5m) long. These traditional rigged craft can be hired with a boom tent that transforms them into a snug sleeping area. Cooking is dealt with by means of a small portable stove and shore side facilities will take care of all your other needs.

Two companies specialise in this unique but fun waterborne style of camping. You can find out lots more on their websites at www.marthamboats.com and www.huntersyard.co.uk.

# Where can I do it?

# 6

In the next few pages we'll be looking at all the places you can pitch your tent and a few where you definitely can't. We'll look at the law for camping and how it affects you, wild camping and whether and where you can get away with it, and a whole variety of different kinds of campsites and how they affect you.

# The law for campers

## Campsite law

In Britain, camping is controlled by two pieces of legislation: the Public Health Act of 1936 and the Caravan Sites and Control of Development Act 1960. The Public Health Act is concerned with tent camping, and despite its name the 1960 Act is concerned with tents as well as caravans and their use on campsites.

By law, any landowner is permitted to accommodate an unlimited number of tents on his or her land for up to 42 consecutive days, or 60 days in any 12-month period, although in the latter case the maximum stay on site for any one tent is a period of 28 days.

Of course, even though landowners have that right not all of them use it and you'll always need permission from a landowner to pitch your tent. The final decision always lies with the landowner. Please respect it.

The Caravan Sites and Control of Development Act 1960 gives organisations such as the Camping and Caravanning Club the right to allow landowners to establish small campsites on their land without the need for planning permission. These small sites are known as 'certificated sites' and are designed primarily for caravans and motorhomes, but most landowners will also welcome a few tents as long as there's room.

The Club encourages all units on its sites (including certificated sites) to be pitched at least 6m (20ft) apart for safety and comfort reasons. This useful rule should not be abused. Do not try to persuade a small campsite owner that there's room for your small tent between other units that are already closely spaced.

**Above:** Watch out for these signs, there are over twelve hundred of them all around the country and each one points to a small quiet site.

# Wild camping at home and abroad

## The call of the wild

Those sensible Swedish people have something they call *Allemansratten*. It means everyone has the right to be out in the countryside. Interestingly this was the inspiration for our Labour Government's recent legislation that

established the Countryside Rights of Way Act (CroW), but the British legislation only gave us the right to *walk* in the countryside, whereas in Sweden everyone has the right not just to walk in the countryside but also to camp where they like within reason, as long as they use these rights responsibly.

Swedes need to ask permission of landowners where this is possible and camping isn't allowed where it may disturb wildlife, farm animals, or especially fragile landscapes. But generally Swedes can pitch a small tent wherever they like in open countryside.

Sadly we view things differently here in Britain and wild camping is generally considered illegal on the mainland. Some people take the risk, and in lesser populated parts of the country you may

well get away with it, but it's not recommended.

If you really want to try wild camping in Britain then head for Shetland. Here it's positively encouraged. I well remember pitching a small tent on a fine headland on Britain's most northerly isles and from my tent door watching a pod of killer whales feeding on seal pups on the beach below. Camping memories don't come more spectacular than that.

If you want to try wild camping in other countries, check out the legislation before you go. In most of them, as in Britain, it isn't allowed, and local police often take a very dim view of foreign tourists abusing their hospitality. You might find your accommodation for the night is a cell rather than a comfortable small tent.

# Finding the perfect pitch

Whatever kind of campsite you choose you'll need to think carefully about selecting your individual pitch. At least you will if you're offered a choice. On some sites, particularly larger commercial sites, you'll simply be told pretty much exactly where to pitch your tent, but even in such cases you should give some thought to exactly where and how you put the tent within the pitch you're assigned.

The things to consider are: which way the wind is likely to blow and whether you can find some shelter from it; and what will happen if it rains, particularly if it rains heavily and the ground becomes waterlogged.

The following are some of the simple dos and don'ts.

Don't pitch under a tree. Tree roots can make the ground hard and bumpy and make it more difficult to put in your tent pegs. Trees attract lightning, and often drop leaves and drip sap. Birds in the trees can drop something worse. Some trees, particularly elms, can even shed branches without notice, so all in all it's a good idea to keep away from trees. Like all rules, this one has a notable exception. If it's really hot and sunny, you may find the only comfortable pitch is the one where a tree shades you from the midday sun.

If there's a wall, fence, or hedge, particularly one that protects you from the prevailing winds, then pitching quite close to it is a good idea.

Although you'll probably want a level pitch to sleep in comfort, a slightly sloping pitch may give better drainage; and if the site gets waterlogged, you won't want to be at the lowest marshy point. Ideally, a soft, flat, lightly grassed pitch that doesn't look like it's the lowest point of the site, nor where water might run through during heavy rain, is what to aim for.

When you find a pitch, check it carefully. Remove twigs, leaves, and any spiky plants that might damage your groundsheet or disturb your sleep.

On many large sites you'll find

hardstandings for caravans. These are not really suitable for tents, but a new style of hardstanding developed by the Camping and Caravanning Club uses recycled plastic egg-boxes. These are buried flush with the surface of the pitch, then filled with soil and a hardwearing grass seed. Once the grass grows, they're barely distinguishable from normal turf but have the advantage that even heavy vehicles can be driven over them without causing damage. These new green hardstanding pitches are suitable for all kinds of campers, but one warning – they can be a little slippery when damp, so be careful.

If you do get a choice of pitch then spend a little time working out the best place to put your tent. Consider the

options above and don't be afraid to take advice from other campers who are perhaps more familiar with the site. They may tell you that the seemingly perfect pitch you've spotted is actually one that floods regularly in heavy rain, and you'll be glad you asked. As your experience grows you'll find, as many other campers have before you, that time and thought spent picking your pitch will reward you over and over again.

**Above:** A great pitch with a view across the river.

**Below:** Woodland camping can be delightful, but avoid pitching directly under a tree.

# Festivals and events

For many people their first taste of camping will be at a rock festival or some other kind of outdoor music event. Thousands go to Glastonbury every year, taking basic camping gear with them, and this and other festivals are now so popular that most big camping dealers will produce a special festival camping kit. A simple two-person tent, a couple of sleeping mats, two sleeping bags, a lantern, and a stove can all be purchased for the price of one night in a half-decent hotel. And after the event you've got the camping kit for future use.

Everything in this manual applies just as much to camping at a festival or an event as it does to holidaying on a campsite. You don't have to rough it under canvas, so think carefully about the equipment you're buying and remember that if you buy something a little better there's a good chance you can use it for future festivals and for holidays and breaks as well.

Despite this, in reality many of these special festival camping kits are used just once and abandoned in the mud when the event is over and everyone heads home.

Another problem is theft. Many a festival-goer has tried to find his or her tent after an evening of great music only to find someone else has removed it and is now sleeping cosily within. For

that reason many people buy a can of Day-Glo paint and personalise their tent, making it easy to find and consequently less attractive to thieves. One supplier, Millets, even produces a paint-your-own tent – the ultimate in personalisation.

The tent industry has also come to the rescue of those who find it difficult to identify their own tents at events, by producing special festival tents in all kinds of bright decorative fabrics. Sadly, however, as with all fashions, you might still find that your Union Jack, tartan, or floral print festival tent isn't quite as unique as you thought it was, and in your disorientated state you might still find it difficult to be sure which of the

score of identical tents is supposed to be your home for the night. Consequently even a distinctive tent would probably benefit from some personalisation. A flag, perhaps, or some sort of windsock flying on a pole could make sure you get home safely.

Perhaps the ultimate in finding your way home is the tent that mobile phone company Orange have developed. Pitch it and go off to the performance or the bar. When it's time for bed, meander towards the camping area and dial your tent's own mobile phone. It shouldn't be hard to spot as it glows with a pulsating orange light in the midst of all those other tents.

## Paint your own

For the ultimate in personalised tents, pop along to your local Millets store and buy their *Paint Your Own Tent*. The two-berth dome comes in white fabric and includes six tubes of weatherproof paint-on colour and a brush.

It's a great way to create a unique work of art, and perhaps, like Tracy Emin, your tent could end up in a gallery with a price tag in the thousands.

# Small informal sites

Because, as explained on page 138, the law in Britain permits landowners to accommodate an unlimited number of tents on their land for up to 60 days a year, farmers and other landowners will often establish a campsite for a brief period when demand for camping is high. This demand may be seasonal or it may be closely related to a local event – a traction engine rally, for instance, or a carnival or village fete. Either way, this provides an excellent opportunity for you to camp in otherwise unexploited locations.

However, some landowners abuse this right and accommodate tents on their land for longer than the law allows. Different local authorities are more or less diligent in policing these regulations and some campers benefit from longer stays than the law of the land strictly permits.

For short stays in high season these small, unregulated sites meet a real demand. Find yourself a riverside pitch behind a quaint country pub – what could be nicer, and if it only lasts a few weeks in midsummer, so what? Just enjoy it.

**Below:** The riverside site beside a Lakeland river provides great summer camping.

# Certificated sites

The Caravan Sites and Control of Development Act 1960 gives a number of organisations the right to allow landowners to establish small campsites without planning permission. Known as 'exempt organisations' under the Act, one of the largest of these is the Camping and Caravanning Club, which has nearly 1,250 of these small sites all over Britain. As well as fulfilling their primary purpose of accommodating up to five caravans on each site the Club also works hard to encourage site owners to welcome tents and trailer tents.

In order to keep standards high the Club organises a competition where members vote for their certificated site of the year. Competition is vigorous and sites work hard to improve their standards. But these are not sophisticated sites. All that's required is that they have sufficient space, a clean drinking water supply, dustbins for the disposal of dry rubbish, and a point – often a simple manhole cover – where chemical toilets can be emptied. Campers will therefore need to take their own toilet.

Most certificated sites offer nothing as luxurious as showers, but they do offer something more, something that many campers find more attractive: they offer a quiet place to camp away from the crowds. A single camper will often have an entire site to themselves.

Most certificated sites are situated on farms and on many of these children will be welcome to join in with some of the farm tasks. Other certificated sites are situated behind pubs, on vineyards, or beside small museums. No two are the same, and with so many to choose from you're sure to find your own favourites which you'll return to time and time again.

One point to note. Because of the way the law is framed, these certificated sites are only open to members of the Camping and Caravanning Club. It's one of the reasons so many campers join.

**Above:** One of the Camping and Caravanning Club's certificated sites. All offer Club members 'away from it all' camping.

# Camping and Caravanning Club sites

The Camping and Caravanning Club is the second biggest operator of camping sites in the world. It owns and runs nearly a hundred of the best sites in Britain and all of them make tents and tent campers particularly welcome.

Amazingly, the Club acquired its first sites, at Walton-on-Thames, as far back as 1913, the year before the First World War started, and it is still running that site today. The Club's network of over a hundred sites now covers the entire British Isles, from Oban in Scotland to Sennen Cove near Land's End in Cornwall. There's even a site in Northern Ireland, in the Delamont Country Park on the shores of Strangford Lough near Downpatrick.

Most sites have full facilities and the Club's holiday site managers have a reputation second to none when it comes to keeping those facilities clean and in tip-top condition. All kinds of pitches are available and campers are welcome to use the many that are now supplied with electric hook-ups.

Virtually all Camping and Caravanning sites are open to non-members, although they have to pay a hefty pitch fee in addition to the rates that members pay. It's reckoned that if you plan to stay on a Club site for five days or more then you'd save the cost of subscription by joining and enjoying the members' discount rate.

The Club has a computerised booking service which is accessible by telephone or on the Internet, and the manager at each site can make bookings for not just their own site but for all those in the Club network.

**Left:** One of the Camping and Caravanning Club's network of nearly one hundred sites. This one is at Kelvedon Hatch in Essex.

# Forest Holiday sites

The Forestry Commission is a Government Department charged with looking after Britain's forests and woodlands. Its main purpose is to grow timber, but it is becoming increasingly important as a tourist industry provider, making some of Britain's most beautiful open spaces accessible for ordinary people's enjoyment.

For many years a branch of the Forestry Commission known as Forest Holidays provided campsite pitches on a score or so of locations, particularly in such places as the New Forest and the Forest of Dean. These campsites were some of the most beautifully located anywhere in Britain and understandably they were always popular with campers. Sadly, however, a lack of investment meant that facilities were not always as good as they should be – indeed, they were sometimes non-existent.

Then in 2004 the Government declared that it was seeking a partner to run Forest Holidays in a public-private partnership, and after a long selection process the Camping and Caravanning Club became the private partner. A joint venture company has now been established with the Club as the majority shareholder, and work has started to bring the management and facilities of Forest Holidays' sites up to the high standards that have earned the Club's own sites such a great reputation. The process will take some years but already improvements are being noticed, and the locations in some of Britain's best woodland settings remain idyllic.

If you're looking for a real chance to commune with nature, to camp in the heart of Britain's countryside, then you should certainly try out a Forest Holidays' site.

# Commercial sites

There are over 2,500 commercial campsites in Britain. They range from huge holiday camps, mainly catering for caravanners but with a few spaces for touring tent campers, to delightful small, quiet sites in beautiful locations. Which kind you choose is very much a personal decision. Do you want a bar? A restaurant? Or perhaps a club for entertainment in the evening? Do you want a swimming pool? If the answer to those kinds of question is yes, then you'll probably pick one of the larger chains of caravan parks.

All of the big chains and many of the larger individual sites issue brochures, and all have websites where you can find full details of what they have to offer, their price structure, and how you can book. In peak season you'll certainly need to book because these sites are justly popular.

At the other end of the range you can find, for instance, a tiny site on an otherwise uninhabited Hebridian island where drinking water comes from a spring and the ferry calls every Tuesday. So if you didn't bring something with you there's no chance of finding it on the island.

In reality there are all kinds of sites for all kinds of markets and all kinds of people. Later in *The Camping Manual* we talk about the various campsite guides available, and the best of these list virtually all the commercial sites.

Many of the bigger sites will carry star ratings, five ticks, four roses, three thistles, two stars, one pennant... you know the kind of thing. Sometimes these gradings can be confusing. Most are based on what facilities the campsite has rather than how well they, or indeed you, are looked after. So a small site that has no swimming pool may never be able to achieve five stars, even if the owners or wardens have made it the perfect holiday spot, and a large but badly run holiday park can still boast five whatevers even though it's more like a set from *Carry on Camping*.

There's no such thing as a best campsite, although most tourist boards and virtually every magazine runs a competition to find its own personal prize-winner. Over the years you'll find your own favourites, and in our experience there are many factors more important than star ratings when it comes to judging a site.

# Sites abroad

Everything we've said about the various kinds of British campsite in the preceding pages is pretty much reflected elsewhere in Europe. France, for example, has hundreds of small farm sites – many vineyards and local cheese makers, for instance, will have a few pitches for visiting campers, particularly campers keen to sample and buy local produce.

The German Camping Club (DCC) has a network of campsites throughout Germany. It produces its own guide and its sites provide superb holiday locations where you're likely to meet and camp alongside the locals.

Some European sites are huge. The largest Italian sites can have several thousand pitches, and this style of camping has reached some new destinations that are growing in popularity with campers, such as Croatia.

The large French campsites, often based in popular coastal resorts, can offer huge and exotic swimming pool complexes, fine restaurant dining, supermarket shopping, and just about everything else a camper needs for the holiday of a lifetime.

However, although European campsites, and particularly the best that France and Italy can offer, have a fine reputation, you may find that some are not all they are cracked up to be. The downside of hot, dry, sunny climates is that pitches can be hard, dusty, and totally devoid of grass. Shade is often hard to find, and European campsite owners will pack campers in so tightly that you may find yourself sleeping only a metre away from the couple in the next tent.

But don't let any of that put you off. A holiday on a good European campsite will be a memorable experience. Thousands of British campers cross the Channel every year, and not just to head south for guaranteed sunshine.

Today it's easy to book foreign campsites. An organisation like Carefree, the foreign travel service of the Camping and Caravanning Club, can do it all for you. It can provide a holiday package with ferry crossings, insurance and roadside recovery, pitches on all the campsites you need, as well as maps and other information, and you'll probably find the price is less than it would cost you if you put the holiday together yourself. The Club offers nearly 200 sites in nearly 20 countries and new sites and destinations are being added all the time.

If you want to, it's easy to put together your own foreign camping holiday. All ferry companies have their own websites and offer excellent prices for crossings. Most European campsites too will usually have a website with virtual campsite tours and real-time webcams to give you a real taste of being on site.

Many campers never leave Britain's shores, but those who don't are certainly missing much of what camping has to offer. Almost guaranteed summer sun draws thousands of British campers to Southern Europe every year. You owe it to yourself to discover the attraction.

**Above:** Lazy Rancho Switzerland, one of nearly 200 European sites on which Carefree offers pitches.

**Left:** Beauregard France, another European site on which Carefree offers pitches.

# More exotic destinations

## And now for something completely different

Although *The Camping Manual* is about family camping rather than rigorous expeditions and adventures we shouldn't restrict our horizons. Tents provide accommodation all over the world and here's a taste of just some of the possibilities available to family campers with a taste for the exotic.

At Addo Elephant Park near Port Elizabeth in South Africa the safari tents are truly luxurious. There's a proper bed, proper hot showers, and a flush toilet, but the real talking point is the balcony that overlooks a floodlit waterhole to which elephants, lions, ostriches, and many other game species come each evening to drink, as well as to excite the campers. There are hotels and game lodges at the park, of course, but none offer such good views as the tents.

It's a similar story at the Pushkar Camel Fair in Rajasthan, India. The Fair, where 150,000 camels are sold in just a week, attracts so many visitors that the hotels just can't cope, and the town throws up a tented village. Four hundred luxury tents offer proper beds as well as excellent bathrooms and the tents come lined with luxurious silk wall hangings. Once again tent campers score over those unlucky enough to be confined to the town's hotels.

There are no hotels on the rim of the Grand Canyon in the USA. To see the dawn break across the awesome landscape you'll need to be in a tent in one of the many campsites that do offer such a view for just a few dollars.

Over the last 30 years the author has enjoyed all of these as well as many other experiences only available to tent campers. Why not join him?

**Above left:** In South Africa's Addo Elephant Park the views from the tents can be breathtaking.

**Above right:** Over 150,000 camels are sold in a week at the Pushkar Camel Fair.

**Below:** At the Pushkar Camel Fair in Rajasthan visitors can stay in this wonderful campsite.

7

## Get out, get camping

So you have read the book. Now you're ready to get out there and get camping.

Perhaps you'll want to join a club? All the details of clubs and associations are in the following pages.

Want to find a great place to camp? The perfect campsite? We'll guide you through the best guides and magazines.

Need to find the best tents and other gear? Our comprehensive directory will point you in the right direction.

The Americans have a great saying. "Experience only starts when you actually begin".

Enjoy some great camping.

# Clubs

### THE CAMPING AND CARAVANNING CLUB

The Camping and Caravanning Club has been in the business for well over a century. Indeed, it's the oldest such club in the world. Founded in 1901 (see page 13), it has over 400,000 members and covers campers of all kinds, from the biggest American RV through trailer caravans to all kinds of tents and trailer tents. Nearly a quarter of the entire membership still camp under canvas, and the Club offers lots of benefits for tent and trailer tent campers. It has nearly a hundred of its own sites up and down the country, all of which provide excellent facilities for tent campers.

Not for nothing is this organisation know as 'The Friendly Club'. The Holiday Site Managers – still better known as Wardens – offer a great welcome and are really helpful to tent campers. On site too other members are always willing to offer a helping hand or good advice – sometimes, it has to be said, whether you want it or not…

And there's the dilemma of any club. Sometimes you just want to be alone.

Your author needs to declare an interest here: I worked for the Camping and Caravanning Club for 25 years. But I genuinely believe that this is a great organisation well worth the modest joining fee. And remember, it's entirely up to you how involved with the Club you want to be.

Many people join simply to get the Club's site guides. It produces what is undoubtedly the best guide to campsites in Britain, *Your Big Sites Book*. (We'll deal with this in more detail in the section on site guides on the page opposite.) It also produces a great foreign brochure for its overseas camping service, Carefree. Carefree sends over 75,000 people abroad each year on camping holidays, mainly to France but also to countries as diverse as Norway, Poland, Croatia, and just about every other country in Europe.

There is also a monthly magazine, *Camping and Caravanning*, with all the latest camping news and tent and trailer tent tests, as well as ideas of where to camp at home and abroad and top camping tips.

The Camping and Caravanning Club also has a number of special sections, three of which are of particular interest to tent campers of various kinds. For a small additional subscription you can join a special interest section known as the Association of Lightweight Campers. This has it's own small newsletter, *The Bulletin*, which is a treasury of expert advice on lightweight camping. Special events are organised that bring together enthusiasts for lightweight camping.

Another special section is the Canoe Camping Club, which brings together those hardy folk who pack their camping gear into kayaks and open canoes. They too have their own newsletter and run carefully graded events, from outings for beginners up to open ocean adventures. All Camping and Caravanning Club members are welcome to go along and try out canoe camping with members of the Canoe Camping Club.

Lastly, there is a section dedicated to those who use trailer tents and folding campers.

### THE CARAVAN CLUB

As its name suggests, the Caravan Club is mainly for owners of touring caravans, but it also welcomes motorhome, trailer tent, and folding camper owners. The Club has a network of over 200 of its own sites throughout Britain and all of them welcome those camping in trailer tents or folding campers. A number of their sites will also welcome tent campers, but many do not.

The Caravan Club also has a network of members only Certificated Locations (CLs), very similar to the Camping and Caravanning Club's Certificated Sites but with one fundamental difference: the Caravan Club's CLs welcome trailer tents and folding campers but not ordinary tent campers.

The Club produces a monthly magazine and guides to its own sites in Britain, but the star of its publication list is simply the best guide available to foreign campsites. The large two-volume edition is the most comprehensive, and in our experience the most reliable guide to sites throughout Europe. As you'd expect, it's designed for caravan owners – indeed, the book is compiled from the reports of Caravan Club members who've visited the sites – but the huge range of sites and countries covered makes it ideal for all kinds of tent campers too.

The Caravan Club has its own overseas holiday service, but again, this only really works for trailer tent or folding camper owners, not those in ordinary tents.

Finally, the Club sponsors a design competition every year with classes for both folding campers and trailer tents at various price levels. Competitions of this kind undoubtedly help to improve the breed.

### THE BACKPACKERS CLUB

The Backpackers Club was founded by enthusiasts for enthusiasts. It produces an interesting small magazine full of technical tips. Events are also organised for those who like to carry their camping equipment on their backs and combine their camping with serious walking.

## Finding a campsite in Britain...

With something over 4,000 campsites available to tent campers throughout Britain and many, many times that in Europe, you'll need some help in choosing where you're going to camp. That's where campsite guides come in, and there's a huge variety of them to choose from.

The first problem is that none of these guides are produced specifically for tent campers. You'll mostly be sharing your guide with caravanners, motorhome users, and in some cases with those who want to rent static caravans.

features around 4,000 sites and virtually all of them welcome tent campers. Sadly you can't buy this book: it's only available as part of the Club's membership package. Indeed, some 1,300 of the sites listed in the guide are also only available to Club members.

Of the commercial guides the *Alan Rogers Guide to Britain and Ireland* has much to recommend it. This is far more than just a list of sites. Each site has been inspected, and there's some personal views on just how good they are as well as the factual stuff. Though the bias is towards caravans most of the sites listed do welcome tents, and if they don't the entry will tell you.

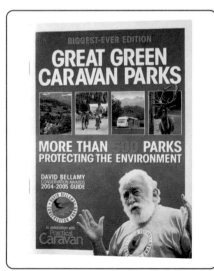

The nearest to a tent campsite guide is the *Camping Sites Guide* published by IPC Country and Leisure Media, who produce a number of caravan and motorhome magazines. Even in this guide tent campers have to share with motorhomes, but at least you know that every site in the guide does take tents. You'll find this guide in good bookshops and sometimes in newsagents at the beginning of the season.

The most comprehensive guide for tent campers in Britain is *Your Big Sites Book*, produced every two years by the Camping and Caravanning Club. It

Visit Britain, the UK government's own tourist promotion board, produces a guide that contains lots of information. However, only campsites that have paid to join the Visit Britain grading scheme are featured in the book, and this means that some very good sites don't get a mention.

*Cade's* is a long-established commercial guide that features a huge range of sites. It's probably the most widely available campsite guide that can be bought through book shops and newsagents.

There are a number of other smaller

guides and many local tourist boards produce their own guides to campsites in their area. These are usually available for free at tourist information offices.

Finally, if you're looking for a particularly environmentally friendly site then the British Holiday and Homes Parks Association together with Haymarket Publications produce a free guide called *Great Green Caravan Parks* that lists the 500 sites that have won David Bellamy Conservation Awards. Again, however, the bias is towards caravans and motorhomes – indeed, this booklet is issued free with *Practical Caravan Magazine* each year.

It's a great pity that many otherwise excellent guides don't realise that not all campsites welcome tents. True, only a few campsites restrict themselves to caravans and motorhomes, but if you happen to pick one amongst that small minority it can really spoil your day! Let's hope that the caravanners who produce these guides catch on to the fact that such information would be very welcome.

## ...And finding a campsite in Europe

Just as in Britain, we've not found any camping guides aimed specifically at tent campers in Europe. All of the guides – and there are some good ones – are aimed at the caravan market, and one of the best is actually produced by the Caravan Club. This comes in two large volumes: *Caravan Europe One*

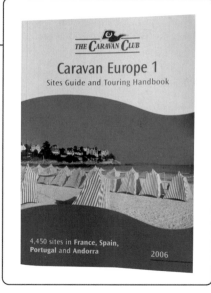

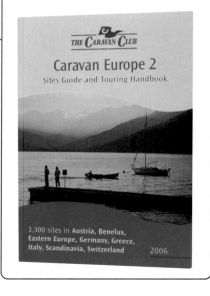

contains 4,450 sites in France, Spain, Portugal, and Andorra, and *Caravan Europe Two* lists 3,300 sites in Austria, the Benelux countries, Eastern Europe, Germany, Greece, Italy, Scandinavia, and Switzerland.

Both volumes are compiled from Caravan Club members' reports on the sites, so they give a really honest view, warts and all. Sadly, one piece of information missing is whether the site welcomes tent campers. Most do, but we'd recommend that you check by phoning the site. As well as site listings and reports both volumes also contain lots of useful information on

the countries themselves, including hints on driving, distance charts, and simple maps.

Alan Rogers produce a whole series of European guides that, like their *Guide to Campsites in Britain*, provide lots in information and reports from experienced campsite users. Individual guides cover France (650 sites), Italy (235 sites), Spain and Portugal (220 sites), and Central Europe (Greece, Croatia, Slovenia, Hungary, Slovakia, the Czech Republic, Poland, and the Baltic republics). There's also a guide that picks nearly 800 of the best sites throughout Europe.

## The Camping Card International

The Camping and Caravanning Club and a number of other organisations in Britain, including the Caravan Club and some motoring organisations, can issue members planning to camp abroad with a special card, the Camping Card International (CCI).

The CCI – still often known by its old name, the Camping Carnet – is recognised by campsites all over Europe and can often be used instead of a passport as a proof of identity. It offers third party liability insurance and discounts on campsites all over Europe. The Carnet often comes with a booklet listing a thousand campsites that offer discounts, as well as much useful information for those camping in Europe.

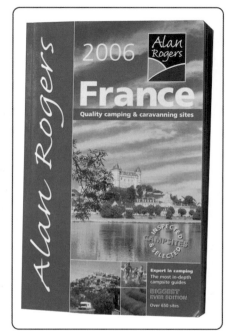

Finally, some campers, particularly those with good language skills, prefer to buy a locally published guide. The Camping Club of France, for instance, produces an excellent guide, and both club and commercial guides are available for Spain, Germany, and many other countries. Carefree, the foreign travel service of the Camping and Caravanning Club, sell a number of these foreign guides for those who want to plan their campsite stops before they go.

## Camping Magazine

The main magazine for campers is appropriately called *Camping*. This appears monthly during the summer but skips a couple of issues around Christmas. It is totally dedicated to tent campers of all kinds and includes trailer tents and folding campers in its editorial coverage.

Editor Mike Cowton produces a heady blend of real adventure camping with more family-friendly stuff as well. There are regular tent and other gear reviews, and plenty of touring articles to whet your appetite for new destinations at home and abroad.

Once a year *Camping* produces a tent supplement that looks at the latest makes and models.

## Camping and Caravanning Magazine

This, the magazine of the Camping and Caravanning Club, is the largest circulation magazine in the world covering all kinds of camping. It is sent out to Club members every month.

Its editorial mix includes caravanning news, motor home information, and a good amount for tent campers. Tents, trailer tents, and folding campers are reviewed regularly, as is camping gear. Touring features make up much of the magazine's content.

## Other magazines

Some walking and outdoor titles will occasionally feature camping or review the occasional tent or other camping gear. Perhaps the one to particularly look out for is *The Great Outdoors* (TGO). It often features camping kit, but only if it's of a type you can carry on your back. Each December the whole magazine is given over to a gear guide, and if you're looking for lightweight equipment for hard hill and mountain use you should try and get hold of this annual edition.

In a similar vain the editors of *Trail* produce an annual gear guide supplement that looks at lightweight backpacking equipment for the more rigorous hill walkers. It covers such items as clothing, footwear, tents, sleeping bags, rucksacks, and other accessories.

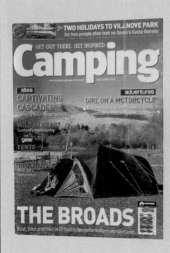

# Codes for campers

## A code for the countryside

- Enjoy the countryside but remember that it's a living, working place. Respect its life and work.
- Guard against all risk of fire.
- Generally, leave gates as you find them, but use your common sense – others less careful than you may have left gates open that should have been closed.
- Keep all dogs under close control.
- Keep to public paths across farmed land.
- Use gates and stiles to cross fences, hedges, and walls.
- Don't go near livestock and leave all crops and machinery well alone.
- Always take all your litter home.
- Water sources and watercourses are particularly important to the countryside. Do your bit in helping to keep them clean and pure.
- Protect wildlife, plants, and trees wherever you go.
- Take special care on country roads.
- People go to the countryside for peace and quiet. Try not to make any unnecessary noise.

## A code for campers

- Always ensure you have permission to camp and always conform to any requests by the landowner.
- Camp only on private land or where camping is officially permitted.
- Never leave litter anywhere. If there are no bins, take your litter home with you.
- On organised sites use the water and toilets with care. Don't ever mix clean, dirty, and toilet rinsing water.
- On informal sites use your own chemical toilet, and if there's nowhere to empty it, empty it when you get home.
- Cause no damage to crops, wild flowers, or woodlands. Always observe the countryside code opposite.
- If you take your animals with you when camping, keep them under control and make sure they cause no nuisance. Keep them on a lead where campsite regulations say you must.
- Remember, campers are guests in the countryside. Respect the rights of the people who live and work there.

# Contacts, useful addresses, and websites

This is a list of contact details for suppliers of products, services and information mentioned in *The Camping Manual*. Today most companies prefer you to visit their website in the first instance and increasingly these websites give no further contact details.

Where possible we give addresses, telephone numbers, and websites. Many of these firms are manufacturers, wholesalers, or importers rather than retailers. They don't sell to the general public but if you contact them they can usually put you in touch with the retailer nearest to you.

We've made no attempt to list local retailers. There are large chains such as Blacks, Cotswold, Go Outdoors, Halfords, Millets, Yeoman, and many more. There are also hundreds of independent retail shops, large and small – every large town has one or two. Find them in *Yellow Pages*. Caravan and motorhome dealers also often sell tents, camping gear, and accessories.

More and more websites are being established selling all kinds of camping gear. If you enjoy that kind of shopping put the name of the product you want into any of the popular search engines and go surfing.

In spring you'll find many outdoor camping exhibitions and sales taking place. They're often organised on or near garden centres or at Scout campsites or similar locations. They're great places to see the tent or trailer tent of your dreams erected, and at the end of the show the display tents are usually sold off at bargain prices.

Also in spring some large supermarkets, department stores, and even DIY warehouses move into selling camping kit.

The choice of where to buy, however, is entirely yours.

## Clubs

### Association of Lightweight Campers
(A section of the Camping and Caravanning Club)
Greenfields House
Westwood Way
Coventry CV4 8JH
*Telephone 0845 130 7632*
www.campingandcaravanningclub.co.uk

### Backpackers Club
11 Morton Avenue, Clay Cross
Chesterfield
Derbyshire S45 9PX
*Telephone 01246 251509*
www.backpackersclub.co.uk

### Camping and Caravanning Club
Greenfields House
Westwood Way
Coventry CV4 8JH
*Telephone 0845 130 7632*
www.campingandcaravanningclub.co.uk

### Canoe Camping Club
(A section of the Camping and Caravanning Club)
Greenfields House
Westwood Way
Coventry
CV4 8JH
*Telephone 0845 130 7632*
www.canoecampingclub.co.uk

### The Caravan Club
East Grinstead House
East Grinstead
West Susssex
RH19 1UA
*Telephone 0800 521 161*
www.caravanclub.co.uk

### Trailer Tent and Folding Camper Group
(A section of the Camping and Caravanning Club)
Greenfields House
Westwood Way
Coventry
CV4 8JH
*Telephone 0845 130 7632*
www.campingandcaravanningclub.co.uk

## Magazines

### Camping Magazine
Warners Group Publications plc
West Street
Bourne
Lincolnshire
PE10 9PH
*Telephone 01778 391000*
www.campingmagazine.co.uk

### Camping and Caravanning
(Magazine of the Camping and Caravanning Club)
Greenfields House
Westwood Way
Coventry
CV4 8JH
*Telephone 0845 130 7632*
www.campingandcaravanningclub.co.uk

### The Caravan Club Magazine
The Caravan Club
East Grinstead House
East Grinstead
West Susssex
RH19 1UA
*Telephone 0800 521 161*
www.caravanclub.co.uk

### TGO – The Great Outdoors
200 Renfield Street
Glasgow
G2 3QB
*Telephone 0141 302 7700*
www.tgomagazine.co.uk

### Trail Magazine
Emap Active
Bretton Court
Bretton
Peterborough
PE3 8DZ
*Telephone 01733 264666*
www.trailroutes.com

# Guides

## Alan Rogers Guides
Spelmonden Old Oast
Goudhurst
Kent
TN17 1HE
*Telephone 0870 405 4090*
www.alanrogers.com

## Britain's Camping & Caravanning Parks
www.visitengland.com
www.visitscotland.com
www.visitwales.com

## Cade's
Marwain Publishing Ltd
Marwain House
Clarke Road
Mount Farm
Milton Keynes
MK1 1LG
*Telephone 01908 643022*
www.cades.co.uk

# Tent manufacturers, importers and distributors

## Airzone
Airzone UK
Pioneer House
Church Street
St Mary Bourne
Andover
Hampshire
SP11 6BL
*Telephone 08701 622275*
www.airzoneuk.com

## Ariel
Hi Gear Ltd
Reynard Business Park
Windmill Road
Brentford
Middlesex
TW8 9LY
*Telephone 0208 847 4422*
www.highgearleisure.com

## Aztec
Burton McCall Ltd
163 Parker Drive
Leicester LE4 OJP
*Telephone 0116 234 4600*
www.burton-mccall.co.uk

## Cabanon
CGI Camping UK
PO Box 373
Newcastle
Staffordshire
ST5 1UD
*Telephone 01782 713099*
www.cabanon.com

## Caranex
Caranex
Cuan Ferry
Seil
Oban
Argyll
PA34 4RB
*Telephone 01852 300258*
www.ukbizlist.co.uk/caranex

## Cath Kidston
Millets
Blacks Leisure Group Ltd
Mansard Close
Westgate
Northampton
NN5 5DL
*Telephone 0800 389 5861*
www.millets.co.uk

## Coleman
Coleman UK Ltd
Gordano Gate
Portishead
Bristol
BS20 7GG
*Telephone 01275 845024*
www.coleman-eur.com

## Easy Camp
Oase Outdoors
PO Box 475
Harrogate
North Yorks
HG3 1ZP
www.easycamp.co.uk

## Eurohike
Millets
Blacks Leisure Group Ltd
Mansard Close
Westgate
Northampton NN5 5DL
*Telephone 0800 389 5861*
www.millets.co.uk

## Force Ten
AMG Outdoor Ltd
Kelburn Business Park
Port Glasgow
Renfrewshire PA14 6TD
*Telephone 01475 746000*
www.forcetentents.com

## Gelert
Gelert Ltd
Gelert House
Penamser Road
Porthmadog
Gwynedd LL49 9NX
*Telephone 01766 51030*
www.gelert.com

## Jamet
Trigano UK
PO Box 3073
Nuneaton
Warwickshire
CV11 4WJ
*Telephone 02476 641140*

## Karsten
Caravan Camping and Leisure
42 Cromer Road
West Runton
Norfolk
NR27 9AD
*Telephone 01263 837482*
www.campingdirect.co.uk

## Kyham
Eurotech Leisure Ltd
1D Croxstalls Road
Bloxwich
Walsall
West Midlands
W53 ZXU
*Telephone 01922 711243*
www.khyam.co.uk

**Lichfield**
AMG Outdoor Ltd
Kelburn Business Park
Port Glasgow
Renfrewshire PA14 6TD
*Telephone 01475 746000*
www.lichfield-outdoor.co.uk

**Oasis Roof Tents**
4 x 4 Touring Gear
*Telephone 01234 742029*
www.4x4touring-gear.com

**Outwell**
Oase Outdoors
PO Box 475
Harrogate
HG3 1ZP
www.outwell.co.uk

**Peakland**
W. Yeomans Ltd
11 Midland Way
Barlborough
Chesterfield
S43 4XA
*Telephone 01246 571270*
www.yeomansoutdoors.co.uk

**Robens**
Oase Outdoors
PO Box 475
Harrogate
HG3 1ZP
www.robens.co.uk

**Robert Saunders**
Five Oaks Lane
Chigwell
Essex
IG7 4QP
*Telephone 020 8500 2447*
www.robertsaunders.co.uk

**Royal**
Unipart Leisure
Parkwood House
Charter Avenue
Coventry
CV4 8DA
*Telephone 024 7646 6461*
www.unipartleisure.co.uk

**Ted Baker**
Blacks Leisure Group Ltd
Mansard Close, Westgate
Northampton NN5 5DL
*Telephone 0800 389 5861*
www.blacks.co.uk

**Terra Nova**
Terra Nova Equipment
Ecclesbourne Park
Alfreton
Derbyshire DE55 4RF
*Telephone 01773 837373*
www.terra-nova.co.uk

**Trigano**
Trigano UK
PO Box 3073
Nuneaton
Warwickshire CV11 4WJ
*Telephone 02476 641140*

**Wild Country**
Terra Nova Equipment
Ecclesbourne Park, Alfreton
Derbyshire DE55 4RF
*Telephone 01773 837373*
www.terra-nova.co.uk

**Vango**
AMG Outdoor Ltd
Kelburn Business Park
Port Glasgow
Renfrewshire PA14 6TD
*Telephone 01475 746000*
www.vango.co.uk

**Vaude**
Chris Davidson Agencies
Unit 6c, Greensfield Park
Alnwick NE66 2DE
*Telephone 01665 510 660*
www.vaude-uk.com

**Wynnster**
Wynnster Outdoor Leisure Ltd
Business Park 8
Barnett Wood Lane
Leatherhead
Surrey KT22 7DG
*Telephone 01372 377713*
www.wynnster.co.uk

# Tent repairers

**Barrons Great Outdoors**
Chapel Lane
Coppull
Chorley
Lancashire
PR7 4NJ
*Telephone 01257 793008*

**Brian Park Camping Ltd**
Unit 1
Chattisham Place
Chattisham
Ipswich
Suffolk
IP8 3QD
*Telephone 01473 652404*

**Canvas Repair Centre**
121 Branston Road
Burton on Trent
Staffordshire
DE14 3DD
*Telephone 01283 541721*

**Cardiff Tent Services**
85a Wells Street
Canton
Cardiff
CF11 6DY
*Telephone 02920 395392*

**CIT Camping**
93a Hersham Road
Walton on Thames
Surrey
KT12 1RN
*Telephone 01932 244311*

**Falcon Awning Repairs**
Lower Basset Down Farm
Basset Down
Swindon
SN4 9QP
*Telephone 01793 814774*

**Kingswood Canvas Ltd**
195–197 Two Mile Hill Road
Kingswood
Bristol BS15 1AZ
*Telephone 01179 601281*

**Leisure Care Tent Services**
Unit 20, Bay 3
Dawley Brook Trading Estate
Stallings Lane
Kingswinford
West Midlands DY6 7AP
*Telephone 01384 293193*

**Poole Canvas Co Ltd**
Cobbs Quay
Poole
Dorset BH15 4EU
*Telephone 01202 677477*

**Skylark Camping Repairs**
49 Devon Avenue
Cheltenham
Gloucestershire
GL51 8BY
*Telephone 01242 262146*

**S. Robb and Son**
3c Cromwell Business Park
New Road
St Ives
Cambridgeshire
PE27 5BG
*Telephone 01480 462150*

**Tent Valeting Services Ltd**
Egerton Street
Farnworth
Bolton
Lancashire
BL4 7LH
*Telephone 01204 708131*

**Trio Pair**
Unit 10
Tanshelf Industrial Estate
Colonels Walk
Pontefract
West Yorkshire
WF8 4PJ
*Telephone 01977 708688*

**West Country Tent Repair Specialists**
22 Ashford Close
Mannamead
Plymouth
PL3 5AG
*Telephone 01752 660317*

# Trailer, trailer tent and folding camper manufacturers, importers and distributors

**Camp-let**
Camperlands Ltd
Mill Lane
Northenden
Manchester M22 4HJ
*Telephone 0161 988 853*
www.camperlands.co.uk

**Combi-camp**
Mangine Ltd
Red Roofs
Chinnor Road
Thame
Oxfordshire
OX9 3RF
*Telephone 01844 214331*
www.combi-camp.co.uk

**Comanche**
Barrons Great Outdoors
Chapel Lane
Coppull
Lancashire
PR7 4NE
*Telephone 01257 793377*
www.camperdeals.co.uk
(Barrons have a number of other branches.)

**Cabanon**
CGI Camping UK
PO Box 373
Newcastle
Staffordshire ST5 1UD
*Telephone 01782 713099*
www.cabanon.com

**Conway**
Pennine Leisure Products Ltd
Chester Street
Accrington
Lancashire
BB5 0SD
*Telephone 01254 385991*
www.conwayleisure.co.uk

**Daxara Trailers**
Indespension Ltd
Paragon Business Park
Chorley New Road
Horwich
Bolton BL6 6HG
*Telephone 0800 720 720*
www.indespension.com
(Indespension have many local branches.)

**Jamet**
Trigano UK
PO Box 3073, Nuneaton
Warwickshire CV11 4WJ

**Pennine**
Pennine Leisure Products Ltd
Chester Street
Accrington
Lancashire BB5 0SD
*Telephone 01254 385991*
www.thepenninegroup.co.uk

**Raclet**
Raclet Ltd
Gorrick, Luckley Road
Wokingham
Berkshire RG 40 3AU
*Telephone 0118 979 1023*

**Sunncamp**
Sunnflair Ltd
Cutlers Road, Saltcoats Industrial Estate
South Woodham Ferrers
Chelmsford
Essex CM3 5XJ
*Telephone  01245 329933*
www.sunnflair.com

**Transcamper**
Camperlands Ltd
Mill Lane
Northenden
Manchester M22 4HJ
*Telephone 0161 988 853*
www.camperlands.co.uk

**Trigano**
Trigano UK
PO Box 3073, Nuneaton
Warwickshire CV11 4WJ

# Accessory manufacturers, importers and distributors

## Aztec
(Various camping gear)
Burton McCall Ltd
163 Parker Drive
Leicester LE4 OJP
*Telephone 0116 234 4600*
www.burton-mccall.co.uk

## Campingaz
(Stoves, cookers, lanterns)
Campingaz Ltd
Gordano Gate
Portishead
Bristol BS20 7GG
*Telephone 01275 845024*
www.coleman-eur.com

## Coleman
(Various camping gear)
Coleman UK Ltd
Gordano Gate
Portishead
Bristol
BS20 7GG
*Telephone 01275 845024*
www.coleman-eur.com

## Dometic
(Fridges)
Dometic Ltd
PO Box 88
99 Oakley Road
Luton
Bedfordshire
LU4 9GE
www.dometic.co.uk

## Gelert
(Various camping gear)
Gelert Ltd
Gelert House
Penamser Road
Porthmadog
Gwynedd
LL49 9NX
*Telephone 01766 51030*
www.gelert.com

## Graingers
(Proofing for tents)
Graingers International
Clover Nook Industrial Estate
Alfreton, Derbyshire DE55 4QT
*Telephone 01773 521521*
www.stay-dry.co.uk

## Hi Gear
(Various camping gear)
Hi Gear Ltd
Reynard Business Park, Windmill Road
Brentford, Middlesex TW8 9LY
*Telephone 0208 847 4422*
www.highgearleisure.com

## Nikwax
(Proofing for tents)
Freepost TW1216
Wadhurst TN5 6DF
*Telephone 01892 786400*
www.nikwax.com

## Yeomans
(Various camping gear)
W. Yeomans Ltd
11 Midland Way, Barlborough
Chesterfield S43 4XA
*Telephone 01246 571270*
www.yeomansoutdoors.co.uk

## Regatta Clothing
(Outdoor clothing and boots)
Risol House
Mercury Way
Urmston
Manchester, M41 7RR
*Telephone 0161 749 1313*
www.regatta.com

## Sunnflair and Sunncamp
(Various camping gear)
Sunnflair Ltd
Cutlers Road,
Saltcoats Industrial Estate
South Woodham Ferrers
Chelmsford, Essex, CM3 5XJ
*Telephone 01245 329933*
www.sunnflair.com

## Thule roof boxes and bars
www.halfords.com

## Vango
(Various camping gear)
AMG Outdoor Ltd
Kelburn Business Park
Port Glasgow
Renfrewshire PA14 6TD
*Telephone 01475 746000*
www.vango.co.uk

## Vaude
(Various camping gear)
Chris Davidson Agencies
Unit 6c, Greensfield Park
Alnwick, NE66 2DE
*Telephone 01665 510 660*
www.vaude-uk.com

## Wynnster
(Various camping gear)
Wynnster Outdoor Leisure Ltd
Business Park 8
Barnett Wood Lane
Leatherhead, Surrey, KT22 7DG
*Telephone 01372 377713*
www.wynnster.co.uk

## Photo credits
**Addo Elephant Park** – p147 top left; **AirZone** – p45; **Blacks Fashion** – p113 bottom left & right, p119; **Brasher** – p111 bottom right; **Broads Authority** – p135 bottom; **Camping & Caravanning Club** – p10, p11, p88 bottom, p89 bottom, p138 top, p142, p143; **Camping and Caravanning Club archive** – p12 top (A Holt), p12, p13; **Campingaz** – p. 86 bottom middle; **Carefree** – p146; **Coleman** – p80, p84 bottom right, p96 top, p101 top; **Cavanex** – p134 bottom; **Commanche** – p 61 top; **Conway** – p19 bottom, p60 middle; **Domestic** – p96 bottom; **Force Ten** – p18 top left; **Gelert** – p50 bottom, p54 top left & bottom, p56, p57, p78, p79 bottom, p84 bottom left, p86, p89 top, p94 top left, p98 bottom, p99 middle, p102 top, p110 bottom left, p113 middle, p116 top, Front cover; **Grainger International** – p53, p55; **Hi Gear** – p54 top right; **Indespension** – p125 top; **Land Rover** – p134 top; **Lichfield** – p18 top right; **Millets** – p36 bottom, p144; **Outwell** – p50 left, p99 middle; **Sunncamp** – p18 bottom, p19 middle, p50 bottom, p98 top, p99 top left, p102 bottom left, p103 bottom; **Terra Nova** – p94 bottom right; **Thule** – p124 top; **Trigano** – p63 top, p115 right; **Unipart Leisure** – p57 top left, p85 top right, p87 bottom, p100 bottom left, p104 bottom right; **Vango** – p19 top; **Vaude** – p110 bottom right, p112, p115 left; **Yeoman** – p79 top, p105 top

## Acknowledgements

My thanks go to my wife Ann, who has let me share her tent for more than 40 years and who still loves the sound and smell of rain on canvas; Joanne Howells, without whom this book would not have happened. Louise McIntyre at Haynes for her encouragement; Camping writers Sue Taylor, Clive Garrett, John Wickersham, Hazel and Pat Constance, all of whom were always ready to answer my many questions; Alec Peters and Barry Norris for their technical expertise; Janet Edwards and her team at the Camping and Caravanning Club, who helped with so many of the pictures; Tracey French for her invaluable assistance with the First Aid Section; and finally to the fine folk of the camping industry. Everyone I approached gave time, advice, answers and pictures freely. There can be few industries blessed with such helpful and friendly people – I thank them all.

The mistakes and opinions, however, are all mine.